100 Ideas for Secondary Teachers

Outstanding Science Lessons

Ian McDaid

Other titles in the 100 Ideas for Secondary Teachers series:

100 Ideas for Secondary Teachers

Outstanding Science Lessons

Ian McDaid

B L O O M S B U R Y

LONDON • NEW DELHI • NEW YORK • SYDNEY

Bloomsbury Education
An imprint of Bloomsbury Publishing Plc

50 Bedford Square
London
WC1B 3DP
UK

1385 Broadway
New York
NY 10018
USA

www.bloomsbury.com

Bloomsbury is a registered trade mark of Bloomsbury Publishing Plc

First published 2015

British Library Cataloguing-in-Publication Data
A catalogue record for this book is available from the British Library.

ISBN: PB: 9781472918192
ePub: 9781472918208
ePDF: 9781472918215

Library of Congress Cataloging-in-Publication Data
A catalog record for this book is available from the Library of Congress.

10 9 8 7 6 5 4 3 2 1

Typeset by Newgen Knowledge Works (P) Ltd., Chennai, India
Printed and bound by CPI Group (UK) Ltd, Croydon, CR0 4YY

This book is produced using paper that is made from wood grown
in managed, sustainable forests. It is natural, renewable and
recyclable. The logging and manufacturing processes conform
to the environmental regulations of the country of origin.

To view more of our titles please visit www.bloomsbury.com

Contents

Acknowledgements

I would not be the teaching professional I am today without the support and encouragement of the dedicated colleagues I have worked with for the last 18 years. I would not have become a teacher at all without the ongoing reassurance of my stepmother, who as a very successful head teacher saw some potential in me. I also have to mention a particular head teacher who gave me a fresh start in her school when I had reached a crossroads in my career. Without her I could very easily have taken the other path, away from teaching. It was her firm belief and ethos that the growth of teachers was fundamental to the success of a school, and that the investment in their skills and knowledge was the driving force behind school improvement. Goodbye to the days of one-size-fits-all CPD!

There are some institutions and individuals I'd specifically like to mention, without whom this book would not have been possible. Firstly I'd like to acknowledge the National Science Learning Network, Project ENTHUSE, and all the companies who support them. I have been involved with both for many years and without them I would not be as passionate and committed to the idea of subject-specific CPD. I'd also like to specifically mention Ross Morrison McGill. It was my involvement with his #5min series of teaching resources that got the ball rolling for this book.

Finally I'd like to thank my immediate family for tolerating a whole summer holiday and many days more of book writing; specifically my partner, for sharing her anxiety and fear for school science lessons, which gave me the inspiration for some of these ideas!

With credit to:

Idea 13: @matthewtosh

Idea 20: @Sally5454

Idea 22: @HThompson1982 https://educatingmatters.wordpress.com/effective-marking-2/

Idea 24: @jackiebeere www.jackiebeere.com

Idea 25: Mia Stacey

Idea 31: Dan Burns www.lghs.net/ourpages/users/dburns/ScienceOnSimpsons/Clips.html

Idea 34: Ross Morrison McGill @Teachertoolkit www.teachertoolkit.me

Idea 69: @chemray

Idea 71: Rebecca Stothard

Idea 74, 82: @agittner

Idea 81: Michael Pinnock @mpinn97owledgements

Idea 83: nuffieldfoundation.org/practical-chemistry/
intermolecularforces

Idea 84: @matgmountains

Idea 86: Nathan McDowell

Idea 88: nuffieldfoundation.org/node/2902

Idea 90: @nateadams

Idea 99: There are many people I could credit for this idea; however, the best examples of this in practice come from @HThompson1982

Introduction

My memories of school always bring back to me that one teacher who got it right. That person was my secondary school chemistry teacher, Brian 'Betty' Thompson. Why did he get it right? Because he stimulated my thoughts, promoted an inquisitive approach to learning and adopted a practical approach to teaching. On top of that, he had a genuine passion for the subject coupled with excellent subject knowledge. I also recall he used to stretch and challenge me weekly.

This book is only a small part of my teaching thoughts, and is a selection of my most successful experiences and strategies from my career to date: a career during which I have had the utmost privilege – to learn from other teachers while in their classroom and beyond. Those teachers range from award-winning practitioners to trainees. They all had one thing in common – a willingness to improve the pupil experience. I would not be the teacher I am today without that privilege.

I recall standing in front of a room full of newly qualified science teachers quite recently. They were embarking on a journey that would change lives and create opportunities. I stood before them and delivered the most important sentence of the day: 'Everything I am going to show you today has happened in my classroom since September.' I had them hooked because my ideas were tried and tested.

I have a passion for science lessons that promote active learning, and one of the favourite pieces of advice I have given to colleagues in the past few years is to think about what their students do other than write. Coupled with this is my determination to get teachers to think about their 'default setting'. This defines them as a science teacher in the eyes of both their pupils and their peers. My hope is that this book will help science teachers improve their practice, and make it easier to maintain a high standard in the classroom on a daily basis. These are ideas, not a set of instructions to follow. They are to be adapted to meet the needs of the individual, and are just a starting point for some stimulation and reflection.

I encourage you to look up the colleagues I have mentioned from my professional learning network mentioned in this book. Without them I would not have been as able to adapt to the changing needs of teaching today, nor to reflect as much on my own practice.

Finally, the end product we seek is not an outstanding lesson every time a group of pupils enters the classroom. To aspire to this is admirable, but to achieve it is unsustainable. The aim is to create an experience for those pupils, for each individual, that leaves an impression they can recall later in life. If you are committed to achieving this then you must explore new ideas and take yourself out of your comfort zone.

How to use this book

This book includes quick, easy, practical ideas for you to dip in and out of, to support you in teaching secondary science.

Each idea includes:

- A catchy title, easy to refer to and share with your colleagues.
- A quote from a teacher or student describing their experiences of the idea that follows or a problem they may have had that using the idea solves.
- A summary of the idea in bold, making it easy to flick through the book and identify an idea you want to use at a glance.
- A step-by-step guide to implementing the idea.

Each idea also includes one or more of the following:

Teaching tip	Taking it further	Bonus idea ★
Some extra advice on how or how not to run the activity or put the strategy into practice.	Ideas and advice for how to extend the idea or develop it further.	There are six bonus ideas in this book that are extra exciting and extra original.

Be health and safety aware: it is every teacher's responsibility to risk assess as part of each lesson.

Online resources also accompany this book. When the link to the resource is referenced in the book, log on to www.bloomsbury. com/100-secondary-science to find the extra resources, catalogued under the relevant idea number.

Share how you use these ideas in the classroom and find out what other teachers have done using **#100ideas**.

Science essentials

Part 1

What is science?

"The systematic study of the nature and behaviour of the material and physical universe, based on observation, experiment, and measurement, and the formulation of laws to describe these facts in general terms."

It seems an obvious question, but we often fail to recognise the importance of ensuring our pupils know the answer.

Start with the stereotypical image of a scientist. Then show photographs of real scientists at work and ask what pupils think those people do during a typical day.

The word 'science' comes from the Latin *scientia*, meaning knowledge. Use the examples below to get pupils investigating how scientists acquire new knowledge over time.

'How big is the universe?' – optics and the invention of the telescope by Hans Lippershey, man in space and digital imaging, Doppler effect and red shift.

'Why are we all different?' – Gregor Mendel's study of peas; DNA structure using x-ray crystallography, including work of Crick, Watson and Franklin; the initial completion of the Human Genome Project in 2003.

'What is an atom?' – Democritus coins the word atom from the Greek *atomos*, meaning indivisible; Dalton's experimental work on reacting ratios; Thomson's work on cathode rays and the discovery of the electron leading to his 'plum pudding' model; Rutherford's scattering experiment; finally the Bohr model.

Studying investigative science helps students understand what science is and what scientists do. Do your school's displays of scientists focus on both the past and the present? The names Kroto, Nurse and Franklin are just as important as Newton, Archimedes and Galileo.

Taking it further

Use STEM ambassadors to get real scientists into the classroom. Royal Society Partnership Grants provide funding for practising scientists and engineers to work with schools.

The big ideas

"Teach, write, discuss, debate, argue . . . all of these should be part of your approach to science."

There is no definitive list of the big ideas in science; this list is from a publication by the Association for Science Education.

Teaching the big ideas is a way to *approach* the content without *teaching* the content. Think of any question you could ask any class; for example, what happens if a caterpillar doesn't have time to make a chrysalis? Now look at the list below. The caterpillar will not be able to pass on its genetic information to future generations; this may affect the diversity of that species and its survival. The particles of that caterpillar will remain and form new compounds somewhere in the universe.

1 All material in the universe is made of very small particles.
2 Objects can affect other objects at a distance.
3 Changing the movement of an object requires a net force to be acting on it.
4 The total amount of energy in the universe is always the same, but energy can be transformed when things change or are made to happen.
5 The composition of the Earth and its atmosphere and the processes occurring within them shape the Earth's surface and its climate.
6 The solar system is a very small part of one of millions of galaxies in the universe.
7 Organisms are organised on a cellular basis.
8 Genetic information is passed down from one generation of organisms to another.
9 The diversity of organisms, living and extinct, is the result of evolution.

Big questions

"Context can make or break a lesson, so make it one that your pupils can relate to."

Think about the day-to-day life experience of a typical pupil. This is your context: their lives and their world.

When you find the right type of big question you have probably found a guaranteed hook. Here are some favourites. Have a look at Idea 16 for some more creative questions.

Why do washing machines last longer with Calgon? (You can get the jingle and adverts from their website.) This works very well for lessons about water hardness.

Is the phosphoric acid in cola good for you? Use this as a way of looking at the safety of acids. There are some great videos out there showing the properties of cola drinks!

Why is Johnsons' soap pH 5.5? Use this during a lesson about neutralisation.

Are baked crisps better for you? Use this as a starter when teaching about vegetable oils.

Does Olay really have anti-ageing properties? Challenge pupils to design a way to test this. Use the small print in beauty product adverts as an introduction to clinical trials.

How did blue Smarties make a comeback? This is a way of introducing food additives to pupils.

Now think about the bigger global questions that are vital to a broader understanding of scientific concepts: global warming, population, household energy, food, health, disease, etc. Use these as big topics with even bigger questions in your lessons.

Teaching tip

'I have to watch TV for my homework!' is always a winner with the pupils, but maybe not with their parents.

Keeping up to date

"Curriculum change is one thing that you just have to get used to in the job."

New national curriculum, GCSE or iGCSE, controlled assessment, modular or linear, which exam board? These are just some of the issues that you need to keep on top of throughout your working life.

The changing landscape is more prominent in educational news than ever before. Not only do you have changing governments to deal with, but also changes in people at the top. 2014 saw a change in the Education Secretary and a change at the top of Ofsted. At the time of writing, the draft national curriculum for KS4 science is undergoing a consultation process, and primary schools are furtively planning for the implementation of the KS1 and KS2 curriculum.

Schools have only just begun to adjust to the move from linear to modular GCSEs and also the change to AS and A2 entries, with Ofqual predicting 'more variation' than usual in exam results because of these changes. On top of that, some subject areas are adjusting to the overnight removal of some course components. 2014 saw 300,000 fewer students entered for GCSEs in Year 10, a decrease of around 40%. Exam boards are currently rewriting iGCSE specifications so they reach parity with GCSEs.

This all sounds like a bit of a minefield until you know where to find the most up-to-date information and how to get involved with others facing the same predicament.

From a science point of view, this much we do know:

New KS1, 2 and 3 national curriculum from September 2014.

New GCSEs in science for teaching from September 2016. No more core science, with the introduction of 'double science' as a minimum for all. Pupils can also take GSCEs in triple science.

Proposed removal of the controlled assessment component from A level sciences. Pupils will receive a practical pass or fail in addition to their grade.

Ofqual are responsible for GCSEs and A levels in England and some from Northern Ireland. They are also responsible for any national curriculum assessment. Keep an eye on their blog at ofqual.gov.uk.

Ofsted have a news page on their website at ofsted.gov.uk/news/ofsted-news/latest. You can also set up an account and receive their monthly newsletter.

The Department for Education have an announcements page – http://bit.ly/dfeanno – and you can also sign up to an email alert for all their latest news.

TES also have a really good news page at news.tes.co.uk.

Don't forget you can also follow @ofqual, @educationgovuk, @ofstednews and @tes on Twitter.

Get involved with, or set up, local subject networking groups. These were traditionally run by local authorities and have disappeared in many locations. Try to get the support of your head teacher first, get the day out of school booked well in advance, and hold a planning meeting. Exam boards are always very keen to come and talk to teachers, as are the major publishing companies. Set up a rota of venues for the year and spread the word. You will find that your colleagues are likely to be seeking answers to the same questions you have. You can almost guarantee that if they don't know the answer then they will know who to contact. Make sure your school understands the benefit of your attendance at this type of event.

Taking it further

A great example of shared resources is the #solotaxonomy Dropbox at http://wp.me/p4cS2J-2H Go even further and set up a communal blog, wiki or shared cloud storage for documents. Make materials available for people to read in advance of the meeting.

IDEA 5

Maintaining curiosity

"The best science teachers, seen as part of this survey, set out to 'first maintain curiosity' in their pupils." Ofsted 2013

This is one of the most extensive reports about science teaching published in recent years. The evidence is based on a large number of both secondary and primary schools, and is a must-read for anybody involved in science teaching at any level in school, from the classroom teacher to the head.

Teaching tip

You will know you've cracked it when pupils come to you with their own questions about science and, in particular, what they've picked up in the news.

The main factors that promote 'high achievement' are:

- accurate evaluation of science outcomes leading to effective improvement strategies
- making science interesting
- assessment for learning
- effective differentiation
- support for learning beyond lessons
- time for learners to develop practical skills.

All of these points dovetail with what you should all be doing day-to-day in the classroom. Now take a moment to consider 'curiosity' and how you make sure this is promoted in your teaching. Here are some ideas gathered from teachers on Twitter.

- Reinforce the idea that science is about the unknown. Unfortunately in school it is often about what's been known for 200 years. @SteveTeachPhys
- Stay curious yourself & role model this to the students. @agittner
- Start with the big ideas, chunk it and get them to map out everything they want to know and share it at the end. @mikecox123
- Use children's scientific wonderings. See 'Working wonders' by @LynneBianchi here http://bit.ly/100ideasmc. @damianainscough

Taking it further

Spend some time in a department meeting asking your colleagues what they understand by the term 'maintaining curiosity'. Also keep up to date with publications from Science Community Representing Education (SCORE) at score-education.org, and look at ofsted.gov.uk/resources/maintaining-curiosity-survey-science-education-schools.

Exposure to science

"Spend some time thinking about pupils, day-to-day lives, focusing on when and where they encounter science."

Two points for consideration here: how are pupils exposed to science and how do we increase their exposure?

Outside the classroom — many agree that kids learn more from a day out of school than a day in school. There are national venues such as the Science Museum and the Natural History Museum, but think too about more local venues. In addition, use local companies for visits. Always include work to be done throughout the day as well as follow-up work back in school. Video diaries are an excellent idea.

TV — there is the obvious and the less obvious. Some examples of science-specific programmes with a pupil target audience are *Absolute Genius* with Dick and Dom, *Horizon* and all the recent series by David Attenborough and Brian Cox. Then the less obvious: *Bang Goes the Theory* and, for older pupils, the more recent *Sherlock*.

TV Adverts — science everywhere! Over-the-counter medicines, beauty products, nutrients in cereals, detergents and cleaning products. The Advertising Standards Agency have stated that as long as claims are 'colloquially understood' it is acceptable to use science that may be 'untrue'; see bit.ly/1ynyeAY.

The internet — pop-ups galore advertising the latest tablets for weight loss. Try looking at YouTube videos for typical secondary science lessons and you'll be hit with adverts for animal welfare, fertility treatment videos and 'The future of glasses — wearable technology'.

Think about how you can use pupil exposure to science in homework and lesson contexts.

Taking it further

@ScienceTVRadio tweets reminders about the weekly guide available from scienceteachinglibrary. co.uk that you can print and display in school.

Common misconceptions

"Not only do we need to know what misconceptions we may encounter in our teaching, we need strategies to gauge pupil understanding at these key points."

Films and TV regularly contain bad science that can lead to misconceptions. These are often just exaggerations of good science that have become common knowledge.

There was once a SATs question with a parachutist in freefall. The air resistance was shown to be equal to his weight. Many pupils therefore wrongly thought he would be suspended motionless in the air, rather than travelling at a constant velocity.

We also have the legacy of folklore to thank for some misconceptions: Newton wasn't inspired by an apple falling on his head, and nor will a coin falling off the Empire State Building kill a pedestrian.

How familiar are these misconceptions to you?

There is air in the gaps between particles.

As water begins to boil the bubbles we see are dissolved air.

Objects exposed to radiation become radioactive.

Heat exists as particles.

Mass and weight are the same thing.

Cells are smaller than molecules such as glucose (this leads nicely on to size and scale; see Idea 49).

So how do you begin to address the issue of misconceptions in your lessons? The simplest starting point is to ask some simple questions and use traffic light cards to judge a response. Then move deeper into diagnostic questioning.

I can't live without . . .

"There are some essentials that every science teacher needs to help make life easier."

This is slightly different to Idea 4, as it is designed to help find those day-to-day ideas to spice up your lessons. These are some favourite places to go for quality resources.

National Stem Centre (nationalstemcentre.org. uk) – get yourself an account and make use of the amazing collection of resources in their eLibrary. They are all quality assured. The 'lists' feature is also highly recommended.

BBC Science News (bbc.co.uk/news/science_ and_environment) – you'll be surprised at how little science pupils read about in the news. It's good to promote science in the news, and often you will find that context you've been looking for.

Nuffield Foundation (nuffieldfoundation.org/ practical-work-science) – excellent resources for practical biology, chemistry and physics lessons.

Royal Institution (rigb.org) – lots of their Christmas lectures are available in full from. Clips from Dr Peter Wothers' lecture *The Modern Alchemist: Air* is invaluable for teaching core science.

PhET (phet.colorado.edu) – Hosted at the University of Colorado is this gem of a collection of science animations. They cover all aspects of science and can either be run directly from the website or downloaded.

Schoolscience (schoolscience.co.uk) – provided by the ASE and sponsored by industry, this is a free website with resources and many links to external sources. It's very useful when looking for real-life applications of science.

Taking it further

If its video clips you're looking for then check out Steve Spangler, the online king of science video clips. Kids love them and they make a stimulating addition to any lesson. stevespanglerscience. com/lab/videos

People power

Part 2

Your default setting

"Take a typical day, with a typical class, with typical planning and typical progress taking place."

Forget about being good or outstanding. Start to think about being you.

What does being YOU look like?

Take this right back to the start and reflect on the following points:

Before you even meet the pupils, what would somebody see outside your classroom? Do the pupils look orderly and quiet?

What does your room look like? Is it tidy, stimulating, organised?

How do you greet the pupils? Do they have a start-of-lesson routine? Some people prefer pupils to sit down in silence and wait, others like to have something prepared for them to do.

How do you set the scene for the lesson? Do you prefer to let the pupils know what will happen throughout the lesson, or do you maintain a level of mystery?

How busy or active are the pupils? Do you always have a balance between formal written work and fun engaging activities?

Are you always approachable? Are your pupils encouraged to ask questions?

How well do you cater for the needs of the individual? Do you always plan for this?

How is the lesson broken down? Consider using the 5 minute lesson plan from the Outstanding Lessons book in this series.

Is the end of the lesson calm, reflective and purposeful? Make sure you can adapt your timing so that this happens.

Building relationships

"Many pupils need a sense of comfort and safety at school. We often focus too much on the curriculum rather than the person."

We should all be polite, approachable and set an example to pupils. Getting to know what makes them tick, their interests, and most of all their frame of mind when they enter the classroom, should be essential for any teacher.

You can make or break what happens with an individual pupil before they even enter your room. Greet every one of them at the door. Eye contact and a warm welcome should be expected as a two-way thing. You are aiming for a positive atmosphere that is conducive to learning from the outset. Don't be afraid to compliment pupils on how smart they look, or that new haircut. If somebody is dawdling, praise the others who enter quickly and have made the effort to get to your lesson on time.

Make sure you reinforce basic expectations. Politely remind pupils about bags, coats and equipment. If an individual lapses, get them to acknowledge that you aren't asking for anything out of the ordinary. Make it part of their routine that they have something that actively engages them from the outset. An example is that having books out at the start means they settle ready to write something in them; whiteboards and an image on the board mean something else.

Pounce on any opportunity where a pupil seems knowledgeable about something. When you get a spontaneous extended answer to a question, milk it. Ask how they know so much about a topic, and make sure they receive praise and reward for their contribution. Get to know their interests outside school so you can ask the musicians how they change the pitch of their instrument, or the runners about interval training and the science behind it.

Teaching tip

Most importantly, stay consistent! Your integrity depends on this and winning your battles at the start of the school year will stand you in good stead for the rest of the year.

Independent learning

"A lot of people never use their initiative because no one told them to." Banksy

Throughout all the definitions of independent learning, there are three common threads: pupils need to have an understanding of their own learning, they need to have motivation to learn, and they need to find a way of working with their teachers.

Try to teach your pupils the SNOT or 3B4Me approaches to independent learning.

The SNOT approach is to get help with your work from:

Self . . . Neighbour . . . Other source . . . Teacher.

Or try the 3B4Me approach:

Brain . . . Book . . . Buddy . . . Boss.

The benefits of effective independent learning from a pupil perspective are improved attainment, improved confidence, lifelong skills and working to strengths on personalised tasks. Most importantly, if used successfully it allows all pupils to feel a sense of achievement. Make sure you provide manageable chunks of work with clear timings for completion. Have a set of resources that outline the required skills in a 'how to' format in accessible, pupil-friendly language. Your role is to act as questioner to lead the pupils through the process.

The benefit to you is that you become more of a mentor or coach during the learning process. You will have a renewed focus on skills rather than a content-driven curriculum. In addition, you will be able to cater for the needs of individuals much more effectively.

Finally, make sure you have a reward for key points of completion throughout the task, along with some quality marking and feedback within your clear timeframe.

Bonus idea ★

Set up a board for pupils to add details of recommended source material they have found during their research, but make sure you also encourage pupils to critically reflect on those sources.

What makes them tick?

"Finding that context, nugget, genre or example that kids can relate to is a guaranteed winner in the classroom."

Do you think like one of your pupils? Take the time to imagine what they read, do in the evening, places they may visit or what the media exposes them to when you're not around.

The following quote comes from *Horrible Science: Shocking Electricity* by Nick Arnold and Tony De Saulles. 'You can make electricity from farts. It's true — by burning methane gas (found in some farts) you can make heat which can be used to power generators and make electricity.'

The opening line of the first-ever episode of *Braniac Science Abuse* was 'The science show where we blow stuff up in search of big answers but mostly just for the hell of it.' This was followed by discovering the answers to these questions:

'Can high explosives make a doner kebab taste the business?'

'Can safety equipment really protect your body from attack?'

'Can we turn a mobile phone in to a time bomb?'

'Can eating bagels make you fail a drug test?'

The first video on Steve Spangler's YouTube *Sick Science* channel at bit.ly/100ideasss was a great Coke and Mentos demonstration.

Now think about your next science lesson. Can you really compete? Probably not, but it has to be food for thought. There are some great demos in this book, and you can always show the more dangerous and difficult as videos.

Teaching tip

Ask your pupils what they'd like to do in their science lessons. Prepare yourself for the ridiculous and impossible, but if you promise the possible make sure you make it happen. They will remember!

Taking it further

For the more cautious of you out there, dip in to *Bang Goes the Theory* for your lessons. There is a great Wikipedia episode guide at bit.ly/100ideasbgtt.

Marble run

"A great team-building activity crammed full of science!"

Very few resources are needed for this great activity for all ages. You can even use this as a staff team-building activity.

Teaching tip

Show video clips of rollercoasters, helter skelters and 'coin sorters' as inspiration.

This activity was demonstrated at the National Science Learning Centre during their annual NQT summer school. It was an example of how something very simple and cheap could be used at a STEM club. You can choose the time limit for the activity based on the profile of your group.

You will be given a tray of equipment.

You have to come up with a free-standing design using only the materials given to you to construct a marble run. The design must allow the marble to fall freely (i.e. unassisted) to the table surface, taking the longest time possible.

Equipment: shallow tray, sticky tape, marble, 30 cm ruler, 5 sheets of A4 card, scissors.

This activity links nicely to work on friction. You can also talk about how traffic is slowed down and introduce the concept of speed bumps and sleeping policemen at some point during the activity. Get pupils to consider the effect of a chicane or a hairpin bend in Formula 1 racing.

As a follow-up activity, video the marble runs and use this to get a more accurate time. Then have pupils peer-assess the videos, commenting on 'what went well' and what would be 'even better if'. Make sure the feedback has a focus on scientific terminology.

Running a STEM club

"One million new science, engineering and technology professionals will be required in the UK by 2020."

STEM clubs can be an excellent way to promote engagement and raise the profile of science in your school and beyond. They can also be a great way of getting pupils to experience science outside the classroom and in a more informal environment.

You don't need to worry too much about the practicalities of setting up a STEM club from scratch because there is loads of help and advice out there. Try the following websites:

Follow the excellent guide at stemclubs.net, run by STEMNET.

The British Science Association's Crest Awards at britishscienceassociation.org/crest-awards.

Faraday Challenge Days at faraday.theiet.org/stem-activity-days/diy-challenge/index.cfm.

Think about who you will invite. Will it be the more able pupils, pupils you would like to be more engaged, or will you use your club as a reward? You will need to think about the sustainability of your club, and this will depend on the people and funding available. Always make sure you have your leadership team on board and point out the benefits of having a STEM club, and make it a collaboration with your maths and technology departments. You will also need to decide whether you run one-off activities or have longer, ongoing projects.

Make sure you have a way of showcasing the work you do. Try to find a space where the whole school can see what you have been doing or, even better, get your pupils to present their work in an assembly. You could also consider joining up with other schools and running challenges together.

Teaching tip

Consider getting a local STEM ambassador involved as an extra pair of hands. You can apply for one at www.stemnet.org.uk/ambassadors/. Longer projects can be easier to sustain if you enter them for competitions and awards, such as Crest Awards.

Primary Science Quality Mark

"The process of gaining the award brings benefits beyond the certificate." Ofsted

The Primary Science Quality Mark (PSQM) is an award scheme to enable primary schools across the UK to evaluate, strengthen and celebrate their science provision.

Teaching tip

Hub leaders should consider meeting with their cluster of schools rather than individually. The science coordinators will grasp the opportunity of meeting with their peers to share good ideas and their successes.

By the end of 2015 it is anticipated that nearly 2,000 schools will have been awarded the PSQM, and there will be 60+ active hub leaders nationally.

The PSQM has the following aims:

- to raise the profile of science in primary schools
- to provide a framework and professional support for developing science leadership, teaching and learning
- to celebrate excellence in primary science
- to work with existing and facilitate new networks across the UK and wider to provide local support for primary science
- to assemble and make accessible a rich database of current practice in primary science.

Schools achieve a PSQM award through a process of audit, action and reflection. Supported by compulsory training and mentoring, they:

- complete an initial audit against PSQM criteria
- decide which award to aim for
- design an action plan which they put into place over a period of two to three terms
- submit reflections and key pieces of evidence (core documents) to support their submission and to illustrate the impact that their actions have had while working towards the PSQM criteria.

Taking it further

Visit www.psqm.org.uk for more information.

All about learning

Part 3

Shock, awe and the ridiculous!

"Finding that hook is often the teacher's Holy Grail, particularly when it applies to a whole class!"

A familiar situation? It's the beginning of September and you look at your class lists . . . familiar faces, familiar surnames, the pupil you clashed with two years ago, and then . . . 17 pupil about to embark on two years of GCSE core science. Or in other words 'We ain't doing no more of that science!'

So, what happens next? It's 3 September. They will be arriving this afternoon for two hours of a subject some would not do at all if they had the option. What do you do? Bang on about punctuality, equipment, and the rest of the basics? Or something better . . . ?

'Is it true that . . . ?' These four small words can change your whole approach to a room full of wannabe gangsters! Out comes the natural curiosity. That's your hook! Give your lessons an element of shock, something awesome, something verging on the ridiculous . . .

For example:

Shock – Should we test drugs on prisoners?

Awe – The average human small intestine is 7 m long. But why?

Ridiculous – What if all the limestone in the world turned to jelly?

The discussions that follow these questions will lead to unpicking the science behind the ideas.

'What if we did build a kettle as big as a house?' Give it five minutes and you'll have all the essentials to work out how much it would cost to heat the kettle until all the water boiled.

Teaching tip

Make sure you have some vivid or graphic images to go with each question or statement. You can find some examples here: bit.ly/1k9ZPiV

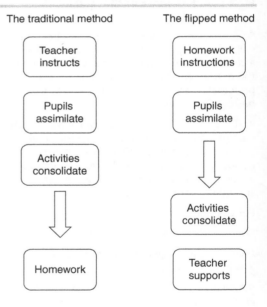

IDEA 17

Flip your classroom

"Turns traditional teaching methods on their head, where instructions are delivered online out of classroom and the 'homework' takes place in the classroom."

It takes a lot of time, courage, setbacks and resilience to completely flip your classroom, but the benefits can be huge. Maybe you can use this with a particular class of students? Before you start you will need to have confidence in the technology pupils have access to outside the classroom.

Teaching tip

Recommended starting points:

khanacademy.org

youtube.com/user/ virtualschooluk

And here's a shortcut to the most popular YouTube science channels: bit.ly/100ideasflip

The traditional method

The flipped method

The flipped classroom concept goes back to the early nineties and has become more plausible with the advances in technologies since then. So how do you flip your classroom? First, it will require an initial investment in time. You can begin with videos you find online, or take the time to record your own videos for the pupils to watch. Get pupils to prepare for the next lesson by watching the video outside the classroom. During this time there can be online discussions about the work going on between the students where they can fire ideas and questions around. You could also set some simple quizzes to complement the videos.

When the pupils return to your classroom for their next lesson the focus is on consolidating their prior learning with activities. Your primary role now is to offer support where there are gaps in their understanding from the outside classroom preparation.

Pros – during the instructional phase pupils have time to pause and reflect at their own pace. They can also access the material more than once (ideal for revision). More class time can be devoted to application and misconceptions. Collaboration becomes a more natural embedded process.

Cons – you will need your own preparation time outside the classroom. Reliability of technology may be an issue and it could be a big shift in class/school culture. The pupils expect face-to-face instruction and may see this as an easy way out for you.

You will be working to create a massive culture change, where there is much more responsibility placed on pupils for their own learning. Selling the benefits and making the pupils feel those benefits is the key to making your flipped classroom work.

Taking it further

Consider using lesson study to evaluate the impact of flipped learning. Have a control group and teach the traditional way, and then take a similar group and flip the lesson. Make sure you can measure pupils' starting points and progress during the lesson.

Interactive teaching

"Picture a lesson in your head and imagine what you see the pupils doing."

How can you get pupils to acquire new knowledge by interacting with stimuli? This is great for new entrants to the profession.

Here's a challenge: can your pupils have something other than a pen in their hands for 50% of your next lesson? As science is a practical subject, it has the luxury of this being very easy to achieve, although you must not drift too far away from the writing about science.

Practical activities are an easy option, but make sure that pupils are learning new skills during the activity.

Give pupils a selection of objects to explore. For example, I have started a crude oil lesson with vials of fractions, plastic objects, images of oil rigs and a petrol station. Ask them to find out what they can about each object, then come back to communicate their ideas. Use SOLO hexagons to develop links and to move forward with cognitive skills. You can see some SOLO hexagons in action on my blog: bit.ly/1Fmj9yk

Take videos and photographs of experiences and pull these together in a presentation that can be peer-assessed.

Highlighter pens are allowed – it's not writing. Pupils can use them to pick out words, phrases or points of view that they find interesting or difficult, and you can discuss them as a class.

Make games or introduce drama into the lesson.

Most importantly, this should not generate any extra workload or lead to reinvention of the wheel. Keep it simple and see where it leads.

Taking it further

Use this during a supportive peer observation. Get the observer to time how long pupils spend doing activities other than written tasks. Make sure you ask for feedback on how effective this is at generating progress and active learners.

Suspense and impact

"Sometimes you need a big hook when the fish gets too big for the pond."

Every now and again try to set the scene with something spectacular and different. It never does any harm to try to reinvigorate a group of pupils. Stretch your imagination and theirs to the limit.

Hooks have been mentioned in other ideas, but this one needs a bit more planning and takes it to another level. Imagine pupils' reactions as they walk into a CSI lesson, where the classroom is cordoned off with some police tape, and an outline of a body is painted on the lab floor. It immediately fires their curiosity. Activities of this type take some planning and resourcing, but the impact is well worth it. You could try some of these ideas:

Have your lab set out like a court room for a debate. Appoint roles such as judge, prosecution team, defence, and key and expert witnesses. This works really well as an alternative to a debate. Get hold of some gowns and a judge's wig!

Use a blackout facility in your department to add impact to the start of a lesson. It always makes video starter activities more enthralling.

What's in the box? You can use this for many topics. You just need a simple box with an old t-shirt stretched across the top; the sleeve provides access to whatever is inside.

Mystery objects always create impact, and the bigger and weirder the better. Try examples such as an artificial hip joint, an old model of a petrol engine, or an enormous analogue volt meter. Have a look through those store rooms for what's lurking in the corner.

Teaching tip

Forge links with local museums and industry and see what they are prepared to let you borrow to spice up your lessons. Perhaps you could source a turbine blade for teaching about metal properties, or an old diving helmet to examine the materials used and how they worked.

What is a tree?

"How do you plan your questioning, and is it intended to be open?"

This idea sprang from a presentation about coaching by Sally Graham from the University of Hertfordshire. The concept of asking open questions, often used in coaching, is just as important in the classroom.

'A tree is a plant because it's planted up and down: it goes down under the ground and up in the air. In the park I saw a 12-storey tree!'

Closed questions are quick and easy to answer; they give facts and you keep control. Open questions need more time, they require thought, perhaps feelings or opinions, and you hand the control over to the pupils.

This idea came from a lesson about the fractional distillation of crude oil. Some pupils couldn't explain why different molecules condensed at different heights in the column. They all knew that this happened, but couldn't explain why. A few open questions such as 'Why do we have states of matter?' or 'What is condensing?' could lead them to the answer.

This approach hands control over to the pupils, and promotes thought, expression and a degree of reflection before they arrive at a final answer. It requires a little more time, but it will deepen pupils' understanding so that when they study a topic such as fractional distillation of air, or separating an aldehyde from an alcohol following oxidation, they can apply their prior knowledge. If they are thinking only about gases turning into a liquid, rather than linking temperature, boiling points and melting points, then they will not deepen their understanding.

Lesson study

"Derived from the Japanese word 'jugyokenkyuu', the term 'lesson study' was coined by Makoto Yoshida."

A collaborative approach to continually improving teaching by examining practice. The process involves planning, teaching, observing and evaluating lessons as a small group. In the first instance, just have a go and do this very informally with a group of colleagues with the same approach to self-improvement.

The process can be broken down into steps.

- Identify a 'gap' in attainment.
- Set a goal. For example 'develop students' writing skills when comparing'.
- Identify ways of achieving this goal.
- Collaboratively produce a lesson plan.
- Choose one person to teach the lesson, while the others observe.
- Meet to reflect and improve, rewriting the lesson plan in preparation for the next person in the group to teach the lesson.
- Finally, reflect on the overall series of lessons and produce a report.

The process is ongoing, and the goal has a focus for up to three or four years. Broader, more overarching goals across school will always take more time than more specific goals. You will need to take this into consideration before finalising your goal. You also need to remember that the biggest investment required is time.

If your school has the facility to video lessons then this may make the process even easier to implement. It will remove the need for all members of the group to be available at the same time when the lesson requires observation. More advanced video systems provide sophisticated accounts and encryption that allow sharing of lessons.

Teaching tip

Set up a system within your department (or school) where the plans, reports and outcomes are shared. If you prefer, you can anonymise all the documents. There is an easy-to-follow document about lesson study by Yoshida at bit.ly/1xlWv8E.

Marking

"Don't let it take over your life. It's always going to be an important part of it though."

You may have a whole-school marking policy or perhaps a departmental one. These provide structure and consistency, but do not forget about why we mark and who we are marking for.

Marking is how you maintain a dialogue with your pupils. This dialogue can be the words you write in their book, how they reply to you, or the time you spend discussing the work. Here are some tips to make marking manageable.

Make your marking focussed – identify key pieces of work and communicate that these will be marked in detail. You may also want to inform pupils what the marking will be used for.

Success criteria – make these explicit, in pupil-friendly language, accessible yet challenging. Make sure pupils have a copy of the criteria.

Targets – targets should benefit future pieces of work. Your priority should be the skills required to succeed, rather than the content.

Feedback based – this introduces that essential degree of personalisation to what you write and promotes constructive dialogue.

Peer- and self-assessment – often seen by the naïve as a time-saving exercise. The best markers will check pupil marking and add their own additional feedback.

Opportunities to improve work – this is very easy to evidence by getting pupils to improve what you have marked using a different-coloured pen.

Stampers – the Marmite of marking; love them or hate them. They can save time and ensure consistency in your comments and feedback.

Learning walls

"More than just a giant display. Use these as serious teaching resources that evolve throughout a series of lessons."

This idea has a focus on pupil work rather than just a high-quality piece of informative display work. You can produce a starting background as a framework to give the display a structure, though.

The key to the effectiveness and usefulness of a learning wall is pupil ownership. Much more than just a fancy display in your classroom, it's more like an illustration of pupil learning throughout a topic. A display becomes a learning wall when it illustrates the thinking process behind the learning of the pupils.

To create your learning wall follow these tips:

- Location is key to success. Those walls on staircases may be huge and tempting, but pupils won't have time to stop on a staircase and read the content.
- Text size is very important. There is no point having something on any wall if it can't be read from a certain distance.
- Planning – get the pupils involved in the design of the wall. Take it all the way back to the objectives for the bigger picture or the detail for individual lessons.
- Ensure that all the pupils feel that they can make a contribution. Know your artists, your technology wizards and your creative writers.
- Try to get the pupils to agree the success criteria and have it clearly displayed for all to see.
- Make learning walls as interactive as possible. This could range from small artefacts that can be picked up or touched to QR codes linked to online resources such as videos, pictures or further examples of pupils' work.

Teaching tip

Remember that a learning wall is more than just a showcase of the best pieces of work. It shows the learning process throughout a series of lessons. Don't forget to revisit the wall and change it throughout the topic.

Collaborative learning projects

"This may seem like a fancy way of saying teamwork, but the underlying structure makes it a successful strategy with pupils."

This was inspired by a document by Jackie Beere about the elusive outstanding Ofsted lesson. There is an excellent resource for a water rockets investigation at bit.ly/1ygKlu2.

Teaching tip

The more adventurous could make all the resources available as shared documents. This way pupils can continue to work on the task both independently and collaboratively. Consider using your MLE (managed learning environment) for this type of work.

The key to making this work is the point scoring system. Pupils are awarded points for completing different tasks on the sheet provided. Some tasks are shaded and are therefore compulsory. Other tasks are optional.

When designing your own tasks you will need to think of the following points: simple brainstorming activities, finding images, watching videos, online research, practical tasks, and presentation of the group's work. Presentation can be written, acted, videoed, uploaded, etc. The beauty of the task is that you can draw on the different strengths of pupils in your class. Use this to form your groups by splitting up the pupils based on their skill sets.

You could consider setting up a whole-class checklist, where groups sign off each task they have completed. This way a running total is available to promote competition between groups. Pupils may look for quick gains or work out which tasks they have confidence in completing. You could also consider signing off the tasks yourself once completed.

Jackie's 'Create a country' activity can easily be adapted to 'Create a new species'. Produce a generic template so you end up with statements such as 'Shoot a video . . . ', 'Build . . . ' and 'Brainstorm . . . '. This gives you continuity in the points awarded for different tasks.

Show what you know

"This is an excellent way of demonstrating progress throughout a lesson and allows all pupils to demonstrate their starting and finishing points in a visual way."

This is really no more complex than a mind map, but the addition of carefully chosen colours makes it a simple way for your pupils to see that they are making progress throughout a lesson.

All you will need to begin with is a set of blue, green and red pens for the class. Start the lesson with a word, statement or question that sets the scene. This could be as simple as the word 'waterfalls', or something more specific such as 'how do waterfalls form?'.

The pupils write the word, statement or question in the middle of their page or piece of paper.

Everything they think they know for definite they write in green.

Anything they are unsure about, but think may possibly be right, they write in red.

They now swap with a partner and get feedback on their original thoughts and ideas.

Learning activities then take place and periodically the steps above are repeated.

The pupils can then draw a green circle round anything red that they now know is correct.

They also add any new learning in blue after each activity.

You may find this strategy useful during a revision lesson, as it clearly enables the pupils to show their prior knowledge and, most importantly, any new learning that takes place. It is very easy to differentiate this activity by having sets of key words to hand out to pupils. Use images with the key words for pupils with language difficulties.

Teaching tip

Don't forget to use a WAGOLL (What a Good One Looks Like) for this activity so pupils understand how the use of the colours progresses throughout the lesson.

Urban myths

"Dodgy scientific claims are not just potentially dangerous; they can be an excellent starting point for a lesson."

Ben Goldacre's 'Bad Science' book sets out to debunk the health claims made in popular culture. Be ready to leap on any sentence starting with 'Apparently . . .'.

Some popular urban myths debunked:

Cockroaches would survive a nuclear apocalypse. Well, they certainly would not survive at the centre of a nuclear explosion, although they have a higher tolerance than humans. However, evidence suggests that the radiation may render them infertile, so their survival may be only temporary.

There is a dark side of the Moon. The same side of the Moon always faces the Earth, so it's more accurate to call it the hidden side of the Moon. As the Moon orbits the Earth every part of it will face the Sun at one point during a lunar month.

A penny dropped from a tall building can kill somebody. Any object will reach its terminal velocity long before reaching the ground. Given the small mass of a penny, you would feel a sting a bit like a hard flick on the head.

Lightning never strikes the same place twice. Lightning tends to strike taller, more conducting structures, so the taller and more conducting an object, the more likely it is to be struck by lightning. Ask the question 'How many times is the Empire State Building struck by lightning each year?'

The important point is not myths themselves, but the badly reported science. You can use more generalised myths to introduce topics such as the MMR controversy, cold fusion, and treating stem cells in acid.

Pens down!

"Think about the time pupils spend in your lesson. Now plan your lesson where for 50% of that time they have to have something in their hand that isn't a pen."

Sounds like simple advice to give to somebody teaching a practical lesson, but when you take a traditional science practical out of the equation there is so much more you could be doing in the classroom.

Here are some simple ideas that do not require much organisation or resources.

Circus of objects

Get pupils to visit each object with a mini whiteboard. Then get the pupils to write down the connections between the objects, and then identify the objectives for the lesson. You could even get the pupils to write their scientific words on the classroom whiteboard.

Picture starters

These can be one image or a collection of images. Use the same strategy as above, and get pupils to make connections etc.

3–2–1

One of my favourite activities that can be done any time during a lesson. 3 simple (new or existing) facts – 2 questions with answers – 1 question you'd like answering.

Lego – see Idea 58

Pictionary

You can do this as a whole-class activity, but I like to do it in pairs. Use a Word cloud from Idea 46 as the list of words to choose from. Pupils take it in turns to draw a word of their choice.

> **Bonus idea** ★
>
> Get a peer to observe a lesson. Make it a single focus of the lesson to time how long pupils write for compared with how long they spend doing other things. Even better, if you have a video recording system, try it out as a department.

The power of post-its

"There must be millions of these used in classrooms around the world every year, but how do you use them effectively?"

Make sure you have plenty of post-its in your room, in a variety of colours. Have a supply that will last all year, and is not just a gimmick that survives for as long as your supply does.

There are many uses for post-its in the classroom. If you want to get the most out of them, try some of these ideas.

At the start of a lesson get your pupils to write their name on a post-it. Then ask a big question (see Idea 3) and give them a minute or so to judge their understanding on a scale from one to ten. Display an arrow on the board and ask pupils to place their name in the correct position on the arrow. You could use their judgements to choose different starting points and activities to personalise their learning.

Ask a question, and have pupils write an answer on their post-its. Get each pupil to put their answer on the board, then take another pupil's answer and add feedback.

Put pupils into groups of between four and six. Give each pupil a small pile of post-its, equivalent to how many are in their group. Each pupil writes the first sentence of an answer on the top post-it on their pile, puts the top post-it on the bottom, and passes the pile to the next person in the group. They repeat the process for the second sentence of the answer, and so on until the piles have been round the whole group. Then they set the post-its out as paragraphs and try to identify the best set.

Use them for peer-assessment activities. It is better to have friends write their feedback on post-its than in another pupil's book.

Bonus idea ★
As a plenary, get your pupils to write on a post-it two things they learnt in the lesson and one question they would still like answering. Use these like an exit ticket and have a place near the door to stick them.

Act it out!

"I love walking into a classroom to see kids running around, being active and learning."

People can be the most useful resource in the classroom, and a bit of drama can liven up potentially dull topics. It's also a great way to visualise the invisible.

Here are some ideas to help you get thinking about your own lessons.

Electrons in circuits – set your desks out around the room to create a route pupils can follow. Designate one desk as the 'cell', and others as 'bulbs'. Have some cards printed with the words 'electrical energy' on one side. On the other side have some with 'light' and others with 'heat'. The pupils move around the circuit, picking up a card when they get to the cell. When they get to a bulb they deposit the card and turn it over. You can modify the circuit by making narrow or wide gaps to illustrate resistance, having parallel or series bulbs, etc. You can then 'count' the brightness of bulbs by how fast pupils can get cards to them.

Circulatory system – a similar type of activity but using cards with glucose, oxygen, carbon dioxide and water.

Rates of reaction – print a set of cards labelled 'A' or 'B', and also have some blanks. Hand the cards out to pupils, and tell them that the As have to find the Bs. Time how long it takes for all the As to find a B. Then increase the number of Bs or blanks to change concentration. You can also give the Bs a number representing how much energy they have, and introduce the concept of activation energy, and then a catalyst.

You can also use Idea 59 on a smaller scale inside the classroom.

Taking it further

Make sure you get your resources laminated and share them with your department. Videoing this type of activity also works very well.

Science in the movies

"Wait a minute. Wait a minute, Doc. Ah . . . Are you telling me that you built a time machine . . . out of a DeLorean?"

Movies are a great, accessible source of stimulation and inspiration for almost any science lesson. Create a successful starter activity using carefully chosen clips from movies, designed to show the wonders of science.

Idea 47 mentions using the opening from *Look Who's Talking* as a way of teaching fertilisation. Other commonly used movies are:

Dante's Peak – some great geology and some serious errors to discuss or debate. imdb.com/title/tt0118928/

Gravity – lots of scope for work about resultant forces and laws of motion. imdb.com/title/tt1454468/

Jurassic Park – evolution, extinction and lots more! imdb.com/title/tt0107290/

Now think about what the pupils actually do. Some simple suggestions are:

Find key scientific words.

Write a tweet about the film.

Think of a headline to go on a poster promoting the movie.

Show the film with no sound and get students to write and record a voiceover for the clip.

A great example is the opening scene to the *Sherlock* episode 'The Reichenbach Fall'. This includes Sherlock in the lab looking at a substance fizzing in a test tube, bacteria fluorescing, indicator turning blue, a powder fizzing when acid is added, chlorophyll extraction. The substances he identifies turn out to be chalk, asphalt, brick dust, vegetation and a mystery organic compound.

Science in *The Simpsons*

"Homer and Bart excel themselves in these great clips containing scientific concepts."

This idea was inspired by a talk from Simon Singh about maths in 'The Simpsons'. Then I discovered Dan Burns' excellent video clips.

Here are the ten clips most applicable to KS3 and KS4 science.

'Skinner's Sense of Snow' – Ned and Homer crash into a salt silo, melting the ice but badly corroding the car. (S12 E8)

'Brawl in the Family' – the Simpsons stay inside during an acid rainstorm (caused by the Republican Party's latest decision to make caring for the environment a felony offence). (S13 E7)

'YOLO' – while wearing a wingsuit, Bart falls faster than the speed of sound. You hear his scream after he lands. (S25 E4)

'Lisa the Simpson' – Lisa finds out that the gene that seems to cause a Simpson to lose their intelligence is only present in the Y chromosome. (S9 E17)

'Gone Maggie Gone' – a solar eclipse in Springfield turns Marge blind. (S12 E13)

'The Debarted' – Bart uses magnets and metal-soled shoes to make Principal Skinner dance. (S19 E13)

'Bart of Darkness' – Bart falls out of a treehouse and takes five seconds of freefall to reach the ground. (S6 E1)

'King-size Homer' – Homer pours oil on the floor and slides across it. (S7 E7)

'Sideshow Bob Roberts' – Homer holds on to a wrecking ball as it demolishes a house. (S6 E5)

'Homer's Check Up' – Homer is given a fat test by his doctor. (S4 E11)

Taking it further

Have you got creative pupils who could make their own science cartoons?

Credit -Dan Burns

Sensitive issues

"We teach what scientists think . . . we don't teach you what to think."

One area where you can trip up is when you are dealing with any conflict in the belief that any individual is entitled to have. Your job is to communicate the beliefs of scientists, and for students to understand how evidence has led to these theories.

Teaching tip

To avoid a heated debate, pass a video camera back and forth between groups. Get them to follow the cycle of record, watch, respond. This way there is no direct contact between groups.

For centuries the scientific community has met opposition from others about its theories. In 1663 Galileo was placed under indefinite house arrest, following his trial after the publication of *Dialogue Concerning the Two Chief World Systems*, in which he defended heliocentrism. Wegener's theory of continental drift was initially met with scepticism by geologists, as he was considered an outsider.

The theory of evolution can be particularly controversial. You can pre-empt any problems by starting with a lesson on creation theories around the world. Aborigines talk about their 'Dreamtime ancestors', whereas the Maori people have Io, who created Sky Father and Earth Mother. The Quran states 'the heavens and the Earth were joined together as one unit, before We clove them asunder' and that Allah 'made from water every living thing' (21:30). You could also think about discussing other theories, such as Intelligent Design.

The bolder among you could introduce debates, but agree ground rules. Try these for starters:

Animal testing saves lives.

Vaccines cause autism.

The Large Hadron Collider could blow up the Earth.

It all started with a 'big bang'.

Global warming is a natural process.

Ofsted

Part 4

Ofsted – what to expect

"Don't panic, stay calm and show them what you do day-to-day."

The current framework for school inspection states: 'The inspection of a school provides an independent external evaluation of its effectiveness and what it should do to improve'. Note that it is the school being inspected, not the teachers.

Teaching tip

Reinforce these expectations throughout the lesson. Don't be afraid to ask a direct question such as 'Why did we say it was important to know this?'

The main remit of Ofsted is to quality assure a school's self-evaluation. A teacher's thoughts will be most focussed on the quality of teaching during the inspection period, and, more specifically, what an inspector will think during the time spend watching what happens in the classroom.

First impressions Try this yourself. Wander round your school before the start of the day and have a look inside other classrooms. What sort of impression do you get regarding tidiness, organisation and quality of displays? There should be examples of students' work, key words and clear expectations. Don't forget posters that reinforce school expectations.

The start Pupils will be expected to settle promptly into their work. Inspectors will look for pupils to have a genuine interest in the lesson.

The teaching Ofsted are no longer required to grade individual lessons. They are 'not to favour any particular teaching style'. Teacher talk is allowed if it generates progress. So do what you usually do if it works for you and the class. Remember, an inspector will ask pupils what their lessons are usually like and will make a judgement based on how well pupils acquire knowledge, learn and engage with lessons.

Teaching assistants It is vital that their role is clearly planned and that their subject knowledge is sufficient to provide the support.

Exercise books/folders It goes without saying that there should be evidence of regular, quality marking with feedback. An inspector will now be looking for 'sustained progress' over time, so there is now less of a focus on 'outstanding progress' in a lesson snapshot. Recent experience of a Section 5 Ofsted inspection saw a relentless focus by the inspection team of 'progress over time' in pupils work. They meticulously scrutinised pupil books, either while observing lessons, or by a sampling exercise. Do you do this in your science department? Do you give any notice? Don't forget they will be looking for pupils improving their work by acting on your feedback.

The key questions Pupils will be expected to know their target in science, their current attainment, what they are learning and why they are learning it!

Most schools will have a process in place saying how pupils are informed of an inspection. Be honest with the students and tell them what an inspector will ask them.

Ofsted – what to include

"Stick to the essentials you know work best. Pulling a rabbit out of a hat isn't what you were trained to do!"

Nobody should be expected to spend all night planning a whole day's worth of perfectly 'outstanding lessons'. It is neither realistic nor possible. You need to teach to your 'default setting'.

Teaching tip

Keep it simple yet challenging! Consider using the #5minplan from @teachertoolkit that is featured in the *100 Ideas for Secondary Teachers: Outstanding Lessons* book.

Nobody is a failure if they deliver what would be graded as a good rather than an outstanding lesson during an inspection. Yes, everybody tries to raise their game, but putting too much pressure on yourself and your pupils won't help the situation. The quality of teaching across the whole school is being judged, and Ofsted will look at other evidence as well as a quick snapshot of one lesson on a particular day.

However, as a science teacher you mustn't lose sight of the essentials when the Ofsted cloud looms.

Context is always a good starting point. It is going to be easier for you if your pupils can relate to the content in some way. How is it relevant in their day-to-day life? Will it be relevant sometime in the future? What will be your hook for the lesson? Don't do a practical for practical's sake; make sure it's purposeful. Demonstrate that during a practical the pupils are acquiring new skills. Numeracy may form a major part of the lesson, so ensure you have the necessary support in place for all abilities. Similarly, there may be a literacy focus at some point during the lesson. Some of the best science lessons focus on the skills developed during a lesson rather than just the acquisition of new knowledge.

Ofsted – know your data

"Quality of data is much more important than quantity. Make sure it is accessible and informative so you can intervene quickly."

Some schools expect you to present data in a particular manner. If not, then you need data that can inform and paint a simple picture with ease. Make sure you get the help you need to understand it, if necessary.

During an inspection you will be expected to 'show evidence of planning', and your data is your starting point. You may have many of the following available to you as headline information:

- KS2 teacher assessment levels for science – or whatever will replace them
- KS2 SATS scores in English and maths
- CATS scores – broken down into verbal, non-verbal, quantitative and a mean
- SEND, Pupil Premium, Gifted & Talented
- End-of-year and end-of-key-stage targets
- Current controlled assessment marks (best UMS estimate)
- -

Look at your underachieving pupils and their performance in other subject areas, particularly English and maths. Perhaps a pupil is also underachieving in maths, and this is linked to scientific concepts.

In addition you will have class lists and photographs. Photographs are better than lists for the next steps. Colour code pupils who fall into particular categories, based on their current attainment vs their targets. You may choose to adopt a departmental approach to this. Remember that context matters and that pupils with 40% attendance will be below target. You will need to demonstrate that you have intervention planned alongside this contextual information.

Teaching tip

Add to your coding system a record of pupils whose parents attended parents' evening. It's always helpful to be able to paint the whole picture for an individual.

Taking it further

Set up a departmental hotlist of pupils who are underachieving. Make it visible to the department, but display it in an area out of sight of pupils. Update it following key pieces of assessment and hopefully see it shrink over time.

45

Ofsted – evidencing sustained progress

"Gone are the days where rapid progress during a lesson snapshot was required. Now you need to demonstrate sustained progress."

The OED defines sustained as 'Continuing for an extended period' and progress as 'Forward or onward movement towards a destination'. Your data may show that this has happened, but how do you evidence this when called to account?

Teaching tip

Take three pupils from your class with a spread of ability. When you have completed those key pieces of focussed assessment, keep copies of their work in a portfolio. If you do this across a department then you can bring the work together to share best practice.

Begin a topic by thinking about the end point or the 'destination' mentioned above, so think of a focussed piece of work that is planned at the end of a series of lessons. Now work backwards and think about the knowledge and skills the pupils will gain throughout that series of lessons. Does your planning make that happen? If not, then no matter what work the pupils produce, they won't be able to show the longer-term sustained progress. One way to start a series of lessons is to think about the outcome and pose a big question at the start that students have to answer, no matter what their understanding of the topic is. For example, use a statement such as 'I can calculate the overall efficiency of a series of energy conversions' and give pupils time to write down anything they know about the statement. After they have been through the lessons looking at types of energy, Sankey diagrams, conservation of energy, and useful and wasted energy, pupils are given the same statement along with a list of success criteria.

Pupils will pick up transferable skills as they make progress. One way of identifying progress in a pupil's writing is to deconstruct a piece of work using coloured pens. Get them to circle the following in different colours: key words, processes, connectives, adjectives, etc.

If you stick to the same colour coding over time then there should be a shift in the use of colours. You can adopt a similar approach to exam questions, particularly if you develop the habit of making them integral to your lessons. The pupils have to write in one colour what they know for sure. They then have a period of helping themselves, and then return to the question with a different colour. Finally they complete the question with a third colour using notes and resources to find the answers. With time there should be a shift from colour three towards colour one.

Your written feedback will always help a pupil demonstrate progress. Think about how a pupil's thinking skills develop. Simplistically, your feedback may begin by suggesting a pupil uses the correct scientific terminology in their answers at the start of a topic. Later on, you may be suggesting that they move on from describing how something happens to explaining why it happens.

Jumping from topic to topic throughout the old KS3 national curriculum topics should now be a thing of the past. Teachers are now teaching more themed or grouped topics, where pupils are working within a larger common theme. So the focus has moved away from a level for each individual topic to assessment without levels. You should be thinking about how you demonstrate that pupils are developing and carrying skills forward during the year.

Think about having an evolving mind map that pupils build as they progress through a topic. Too often these great tools are restricted to the end of a topic as a revision activity. You can influence the quality and usefulness of these by providing a basic structure with some essential categories. An example for metal extraction could include a reactivity series, ores, methods of extraction, displacement/redox and details of particular metals. You could also add a context section with space for 'issues'.

Taking it further

Use command words and Bloom's taxonomy to show progress in the questions and tasks you give to pupils. This is a guaranteed way to show progress and the wording you use will shift towards higher-order thinking skills as time moves on.

Ofsted – they talk to pupils

"Pupils' views are gathered through discussions with groups of pupils selected by the inspection team."

You can expect an inspector to talk to pupils in the classroom, or even take a small group outside to speak to them in more depth. This is in addition to pupil questionnaires.

The best advice for approaching this eventuality is to make sure you keep hold of the general idea that you let Ofsted see what you do day-to-day. Don't set yourself up for a big fail by changing that 'default setting' during an inspection. Be prepared for pupils to be asked the following:

What are you learning today? You will have made your objectives clear anyway.

Why are you learning this? The importance of context and relating the science to pupils' everyday lives will address this.

What do you know now that you didn't know at the start of the lesson? This is an easy one to tackle if you have very explicit success criteria and/or outcomes that pupils periodically revisit.

What do you need to do to move up to the next step? Again, your success criteria will dictate this, whether it is linked to levels, grades or skills.

What is a typical science lesson usually like? Try to instil a sense of being scientists in your pupils. You want more than 'we do lots of practical work' as their answer. Wouldn't it be great for pupils to respond with 'we usually start with a big picture (literally) and discuss what it all means to us'. Think about the impression that will make!

How well are you doing in science at the moment? Ideally pupils will refer to targets, current attainment and details about how they can improve. An inspector will leave with a feeling of confidence if pupils are able to communicate this way.

Taking it further

Use the points given as a volunteered lesson observation focus. Ask somebody to take a few pupils outside and try out these questions. Use it as a way of collecting some very personalised pupil voice evidence, and, most importantly, acting upon it.

Literacy

Part 5

Scientific literacy

"Scientific literacy allows people to evaluate scientific sources of information, giving them confidence to scrutinise science."

The biggest change in recent years is how pupils are exposed to science in the media — fewer books and newspapers and more online content.

Teaching tip

Talking about science is just as important as writing about science as a way of getting pupils to communicate their understanding of scientific work.

How do we define scientific literacy? There is no clear definition of the term, but the American Association for the Advancement of Science says 'When people know how scientists go about their work and reach scientific conclusions, and what the limitations of such conclusions are, they are more likely to react thoughtfully to scientific claims and less likely to reject them out of hand or accept them uncritically.'

The OECD PISA draft science framework 2015 outlines three competencies for assessing scientific literacy, at bit.ly/100ideaspisa:

1 Explain Phenomena Scientifically

2 Evaluate and Design Scientific Enquiry

3 Interpret Data and Evidence Scientifically

Suggestions for promoting literacy skills:

Books – *Horrible Science (or anything on the* Royal Society's Young People's Book Prize list at royalsociety.org/awards/young-people)

CBBC – *Absolute Genius, Brain Freeze, Fierce Earth, Richard Hammond's Miracles of Nature*

BBC – *Horizon, The Sky at Night*

YouTube channels – *MinutePhysics, The Science Channel, SciShow, Vsauce, TheSpanglerEffect, Doctor Mad Science, Bill Nye the Science Guy*

Magazines – *BBC Focus, Cosmos, How it Works*

Writing to compare

"This style of writing is usually objective but it may also be subjective. It is crucial that pupils read the question and identify what is required of them."

Comparison is perhaps a little more complicated than just identifying the similarities and differences between objects. Older pupils may be looking at the opinions of two sides in an argument. The starting point is a structure for pupils to identify what they are comparing and then to build on it.

Begin with a graphic organiser as mentioned in Idea 42. The same type can be used for any age or ability of pupils. The simplest type consists of two overlapping circles, as at bit.ly/100ideascom. Instead of using a graphic organiser, you could just use three coloured pens for 'item 1 differences', 'in common', 'item 2 differences'.

Now think about a catchy context to begin with. Teenagers can very easily compare an Xbox with a PlayStation, or an iPhone with an Android phone, so begin within their comfort zone. Get them to identify for themselves what sort of language they are using. Show them an example on the board and see if they can pick out the common language between that piece and their own.

The connectives required will either indicate equality (coordination) or inequality (subordination).

Coordination: also, just as, similarly, moreover, likewise.

Subordination: although, however, instead, rather than, unlike, on the other hand, whereas.

Finally, don't forget those adverbs. Make sure your pupils are using comparatives such as larger, bigger and dirtier, as well as superlatives such as largest, biggest and dirtiest.

Teaching tip

The more complex, but just as easy to use, version of the overlapping circles diagram can be found at bit.ly/100ideascom2. This version is better suited to older pupils and is a good starting point for a piece of writing.

Bonus idea

Look online for a review of the latest version of a gadget such as a phone or tablet. You will usually be able to find out how it compares to the previous version and what has changed. Make sure pupils can identify the language of comparison.

Writing to describe

"Paint a vivid picture in the reader's head."

The key to developing this style of scientific writing is to make sure pupils concentrate on the senses. In addition, they will need to use the most suitable adverbs and adjectives.

Teaching tip

A key skill is being able to describe what has happened from either a table of results or a graph. Make sure pupils understand the concept of gradients, as well as horizontal and vertical lines.

Far too often pupils confuse the 'what' with the 'why'. To help students describe a situation you will need to draw on their imagination. Get them to draft work on whiteboards. There is a memorable scene in *Dead Poets' Society* where Mr Keating gets shy Todd to recite a poem to the whole class. Only when Todd is forced to close his eyes does he truly express himself. Try this yourself by getting pupils to close their eyes and tell a friend what just happened.

- Have pupils sit in silence and write down what they hear.
- Show a set of objects on the board for a minute and get pupils to write down what they are. Make sure you have the same items in different colours and/or sizes.
- Use video clips of situations or experiments for pupils to describe. Get the pupils to change the adverbs and adjectives used in their first draft.
- Put an adverb/adjective on the board and ask for alternatives. For example 'the reaction began quickly' sounds so much better if we use rapidly, immediately, instantly, promptly or instantaneously.

Use coloured pens to get pupils to annotate all the verbs, adverbs, nouns and adjectives in a passage of descriptive text. Then move on to pupils doing the same to their own draft work. The final version of their work should demonstrate higher-level language skills, and is a great way of demonstrating that pupils are making progress.

Creative writing

"Set pupils free to express themselves within their comfort zone. Allow them to demonstrate their talents in other areas and be prepared to be amazed."

Bring scientific ideas to life by exploring them through creative writing. Looking at a process from a different point of view is a great way to aid memory of the process.

There are plenty of areas of science perfect for this genre, particularly topics that include a sequence of events. You can have a focus for the writing such as connectives, adjectives, adverbs or similes.

A great creative starter is the opening scene from the film *Look Who's Talking*. It fits perfectly into a reproduction topic and is a great way for pupils to write about the process of fertilisation. The clip can be found here: bit.ly/100ideaslwt

Try getting pupils to write about the journey of a cheese sandwich as it travels through the digestive system. Lower key stages could concentrate on the parts of the body; older pupils can describe encounters with enzymes.

Take a 'bucket full of joules' and write about what happens when the water is lifted to a height and allowed to travel downhill. It could pass through a turbine or end up in the sea as part of a wave or the tide. You could miss out the middle completely and just define an ending such as a light bulb turning on. It's a great way to get the pupils writing about energy transfers.

Other ideas: Look out for 'Harry the Hydrocarbon' lurking in your prep room, where he is talking about his journey through an oil refinery, or use the virtual refinery tour at bit.ly/1K27ytK

Teaching tip

Be creative with how you display the finished work. Pollination 'through the eyes of a bee' could be displayed with the writing inside the petals of a giant flower. You could go as far as a Prezi presentation on a touch screen.

Graphic organisers

"I've been using these for a long time, and my favourites are available as laminated sets that can be ordered when required."

The 'spider diagram' is a graphic organiser, as it provides a very simple structure for a task. Here are some suggestions for how to use different types in your science lessons. You can also think of the #5minprac as a very specialised example.

Venn diagram – for similarities and differences. More advanced versions could have three overlapping circles. You could use these for comparing different species.

Continuum – for timelines, etc.

Cycle – lime cycle, menstrual cycle, etc.

Sequencing – for the logical sequence of events such as a reflex arc, or fractional distillation.

Cluster – what you will usually visualise as a mind map.

Fishbone – useful for cause and effect for more complex activities.

Ladder – for ranking activities such as reactivity series.

Chain of overlapping rings – the overlap states how the two rings are connected and can be an extension of a sequencing activity.

Droplets – for collecting ideas at the start of a lesson.

You will find a graphic organiser a great way of keeping pupils focussed if they are watching video clips. I often use a very simple sheet divided into quarters for what, why, how, etc. Use a template you have saved and just change the words in the boxes to suit the activity.

Homophones, homonyms and homographs

"Bohr was bored by the bored boar!"

The Chinese don't have words with multiple meanings, so there isn't any confusion like we encounter in the English language.

Homophones – words that sound the same but have different spellings. He blew out the blue candle.

Homonyms – same spelling and pronunciation but different meanings. It was a fair price for the ride at the fair.

Homographs – words that are spelt the same but have different pronunciation and meanings. An archer's bow and the bow of a boat [a tree has a bough!].

Many of you will now be teaching many more EAL (English as an additional language) pupils, or perhaps new entrants to the country with no English whatsoever. How do you develop strategies to help pupils develop their scientific literacy? Think about these pairs of words: meter and metre, sun and son, iron and ion, lever and leaver, current and currant. Now consider the words iron, fly, bulb, conductor and cell.

You need to make your lessons as visual as possible to enable pupils to access the scientific language required to succeed in class. A simple diagram of a metre rule next to an electricity meter will suffice, but this can be time consuming. Have pupils repeat sentences back to each other and, for homophones, have them point to the correct spelling on a whiteboard as they say the word. For homographs have pupils act out the word. So for metre they widen their arms to a metre wide, and for a meter they move their arm like a dial.

Teaching tip

Have pupils make their own dictionary of scientific words that they build up lesson by lesson. There are also some very useful scientific dictionaries out there for your EAL pupils.

In the news

"Well, news is anything that's interesting, that relates to what's happening in the world, what's happening in areas of the culture that would be of interest to your audience." Kurt Loder, American journalist, b. 1945

What science stories are hitting the headlines, and what are their curriculum links?

NASA rover to make oxygen on Mars – solar system, chemical reactions.

Dinosaurs 'shrank' to become birds – evolution.

Minister wants end to animal testing – ethics, development of drugs.

Tablet screens to correct sight loss – optics.

Heart attack on a plate? The truth about saturated fat – healthy eating, hydrocarbons.

Largest ever Ebola outbreak is not a global threat – viruses, vaccinations.

Once you have found your captivating news story, what can you do next? Here are some tips for getting pupils engaged in their learning:

Get older pupils to rewrite the story for a younger reading age. Have them identify the key concepts, processes and words. Perhaps produce a writing frame to help structure the article.

Turn the written news article into a news report. Have the students use a filmstrip from Idea 47 to plan the filming.

Turn the news story into a display. This could be a larger group activity where pupils work on a specific aspect of the story.

This is an ideal opportunity to get pupils to understand the importance of reputable sources. Introduce the concept of 'bias' and 'vested interest' at this point.

Taking it further

A great current topic for this is fracking. You could also introduce the concept of 'peer-review' and the MMR controversy.

Talk about it!

"How often do you just allow pupils time to talk about something? Is it encouraged by you, or are you afraid to just let them go?"

Before taking answers to a question, simply tell the pupils to just 'talk about it' so they can share and develop their ideas.

Where can this very rich strategy take you? Possibly out of both your own comfort zone and that of the pupils. Perhaps you aren't confident enough to let go of the control you have over when pupils can talk. However, some pupils can communicate their ideas much better if they're not sitting wondering if you will choose them to answer the question. Just a few minutes discussing a question with carefully created groups will enable individuals to develop their answer and grow in confidence.

This can be a great starter when the question you introduce the lesson with is the focus of the lesson. It could be a 'big question', or just something small and specific to set the scene for what follows. It is an effective technique to address misconceptions, with questions such as 'What happens if we heat . . . ?' You could develop this further by giving groups different questions to talk about, then mixing up the groups and getting them to share their discussion points.

Consider taking small groups of students out of lessons to hold 'learning discussions'. You lead the students through some prior learning by allowing them to share their ideas in an informal environment. The key to success is how you lead pupils through the discussion. It's a great way of unpicking misconceptions.

Teaching tip

Give one group member a whiteboard to record key words that are used during the conversation. Make it a competition to see which group can create the longest list.

Word clouds

"Get to grips with key words and enhance pupil literacy skills."

All you need is a passage of text or a list of key words and you're off in minutes with a word cloud in the classroom.

Here's how to begin. First, you will need a passage of text or a list of the words you'd like to use. If you use a passage of text then the size of the word that appears in your word cloud is proportional to the frequency of the word in the text. All you have to do is paste the passage in to a word cloud generator, such as the one at wordle.net/create. You can modify the settings of your word cloud to change the font and colours. One of the most useful tools in Wordle is the option to choose how many words to include in your word cloud.

The example below was generated using the text from a GCSE specification.

Ideas for using your word cloud:

- Pick out the ten most important words.
- Can you link pairs of words?
- Write sentences containing pairs of words.
- Write sentences linking more than two words.
- What are the lesson objectives?
- Write questions you'd like answering based on the words you see.

Taking it further

If you're a fan of #SOLO taxonomy, use laminated hexagons to group and make connections between words.

Filmstrip science

"Bring out the creative side of your pupils with a fun visual activity they can all succeed at!"

Use very simple filmstrips for lots of different scenarios. They can be an effective starting point to help pupils scaffold a piece of follow-up writing.

This approach is very effective with pupils of all ages and abilities. Use a simple template like the one below; there are loads of these available online.

Filmstrips work well for processes that are a 'sequence of events'. A great lesson for this activity is teaching fertilisation using the opening scene from the film *Look Who's Talking*. Another example is the journey of a hot-air balloon. Pupils draw a series of pictures showing the density of the air particles both inside and outside the balloon.

It can also be used for practical activities that happen in steps. Try it for separating salt from rock salt, the steps involved in titration, preparing a bacterial culture, the forces acting on a freefall parachutist and the processes involved from fertilisation to birth. You can also use it for planning stop-motion activities, like the one mentioned in Idea 58.

Get pupils to use their filmstrips to turn the steps in to a piece of writing using connectives. You could also get pupils to make videos of their steps, or turn them in to a presentation.

A sequence of events

"Many concepts in core science are based on a logical sequence of events. Being able to write about these is always easier if the correct connectives are used."

You can use this to help pupils structure their answers. This naturally links to Idea 98 6 mark questions. Having the right tools is vital for exam success.

AQA used this instruction as part of their 6-mark questions – 'In this question you will be assessed on using good English, organising information clearly and using specialist terms where appropriate.' They also noted in a recent examiner's report that, when 6 marks were awarded, 'students paid close attention to the quality of their written responses as well as to the scientific content. Answers to questions like these should be well-organised . . . '

The following are GCSE core science examples of common sequences of events:

- aseptic technique
- vaccinations
- responding to stimuli
- menstrual cycle
- testing new drugs
- carbon cycle
- adult cell cloning
- lime cycle
- phytomining
- fractional distillation oil/air
- ethanol production
- electricity generation.

Your pupils need to be aware of their sequencing connectives: first, second (etc), finally, hence, next, then, from here on, to begin with, last of all, after, before, as soon as, in the end, gradually. You can adopt many strategies to cater for different needs.

Consider giving less able pupils the list of events as a card sort. You can make this even easier if you design it as a cut-up jigsaw puzzle. You may also find it useful to leave spaces to allow pupils to choose the appropriate connectives. If you're feeling more adventurous, you can design interactive drag and drop activities, either for PowerPoint or for your whiteboard software.

Try this simple group activity to get pupils started. Arrange the pupils in a circle and hand each person a piece of paper with the first line of the sequence at the top. Each pupil writes the next step in the sequence. They can then either pass it on to the next person, or fold over the first line and pass it on with just the second line showing. Any pupil who can't go any further drops out; the remaining pupils carry on with their sequences. You can use a sequencing graphic organiser to help your pupils to draft their work.

Taking it further

Do this as a speaking and listening activity. Begin by getting pupils to create a random story, with each person continuing where the last person left off. Then apply the same skill to the science.

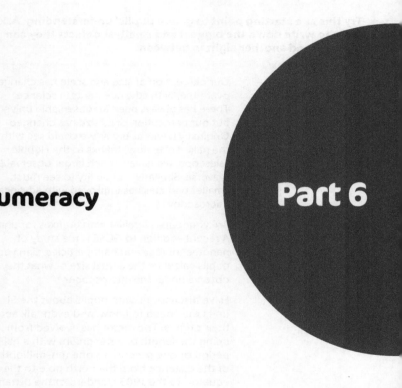

Numeracy

Part 6

Size and scale

"This is the first mathematical requirement of one of the major exam boards. It is important in all areas of science at all key stages."

Try this as a starting point to gauge pupils' understanding. Ask them to write down the biggest and smallest objects they can think of, and another eight in between.

Teaching tip

Use this scale of the universe animation in your lessons. It never fails to fascinate pupils. htwins. net/scale2/

Our perception of size and scale has changed over time, with advancements in science. There has always been an observable universe, but our perception of its size has changed. Originally it was as big as we could see with the naked eye; now, thanks to the Hubble telescope, we have a much larger observable universe. Similarly, our ability to see much smaller particles has improved with advances in microscopy.

Are your pupils familiar with prefixes for units? A recent addition to GCSE is the study of nanotechnology and nanoparticles. Can your pupils calculate the actual size of what they observe under the microscope?

Have discussions with pupils about the SI units they need to know, and even talk about their origins. The metre has evolved from being the length of a pendulum with a half-period of one second, to one ten-millionth of the distance from the north pole to the equator, to the 1983 standard of the distance light travels in 1/299,792,458 of a second, for example.

The next time you are building scale models of the solar system, looking at the structure of an atom, or discussing the sizes of bacteria, viruses and fungi, take time to develop pupils' understanding of the actual sizes of what they are studying.

The language of measurement

"Is it reliable, repeatable or reproducible?"

With the many changes to the curriculum and specification in recent years, there has been much change in terminology.

The 2015 KS3 National Curriculum states that pupils should be able to 'make and record observations and measurements using a range of methods for different investigations; and evaluate the reliability of methods and suggest possible improvements'. At KS4 they should be 'making and recording observations and measurements using a range of apparatus and methods' and 'having due regard to . . . the accuracy of measurements'.

Ask a pupil for the time, and see what happens. Chances are that you won't get an answer that includes seconds. Have a selection of different clocks to illustrate the concept of precision. Now ask pupils how we know what the real time actually is!

Challenge pupils to measure out 100 cm³ of water using different pieces of equipment to introduce scale divisions. Blindfold pupils and give them a pen and a piece of paper with a target in the middle. Ask them to put ten dots on the paper. Have a discussion about the pattern of dots using the words accurate, precise and repeatable.

Accuracy – how close to the real value.

Precision – closeness of agreement between measured values.

Repeatable – ability of one user to get the same measurement under the same conditions.

Reproducible – ability of other to get the same measurements under equivalent conditions.

> **Teaching tip**
>
> The ASE (Association for Science Education) produced an excellent publication about the language of measurement. It is available from bit. ly/140Tzmn.

Line graphs

"That's not how we do them in maths!!"

This is always a controversial, frustrating and emotive issue. So, let's get the main points out in the open and consider some approaches that will work in the classroom without too much preparation. Essential for controlled assessment at GCSE and beyond . . .

First you have to make sure that pupils understand that a line graph can be produced only if the independent and dependent variables are both continuous. This means they can take any value between a minimum and maximum. For example, a car can travel from standstill to, say, 70 km/h and could also travel at any velocity between these two values.

Next we have to ensure that pupils understand that their graph could show:

- a straight line (possibly through the origin)
- a smooth curve
- no correlation.

Step 1

Give the pupils just a results table, with no headings or units, just numbers. Get them to try to draw a graph of just the points and/or line. Consider asking for a sketch graph and banning any scales.

Step 2

Create a list of possible scenarios. You are going to ensure that pupils have an appreciation of scale so they can begin to recognise just how important the numbers are at the start. Ask pupils to draw labelled axes with maximum values, then break the axes down with a smaller scale.

- Hand span vs height – up to 20 cm and up to 200 cm.
- Mass of car vs top speed – up to 3,000 kg and 300 km/h.

Step 3

Have some pre-printed scales that pupils can place on graph paper. Produce them for both *x* and *y* axes. Give pupils more scenarios, with results this time, and get pupils to choose the correct scales for the given results and try to produce a graph. Introduce labelling axes with units at this point.

Step 4

Pupils have to produce their own scales for scenarios that have results provided. They then add points to the graph after adding the scale and labels.

You can score a graph out of 4 using these criteria:

1 Both axes labelled with units.
2 Appropriate scale on both axes.
3 Points plotted +/- half a square tolerance.
4 Appropriate line or no correlation.

Taking it further

Try to source some gingham-print wipeable table cloth – usually sold on a roll by the metre. It's great for a huge display on the wall, has squares all over it, and you can annotate it, change it and even produce some strips with scales as mentioned in the main idea.

Graphs, correlations and other stuff

"Time to sort out once and for all the relationship between two sets of numbers plotted on a graph."

The relationships need reinforcing from the outset, with annotations on every graph a pupil produces or encounters.

Use examples of graphs and get pupils to describe the relationships they can see. Try to catch students out by drawing a poor line of best fit, or forgetting to ignore anomalies.

No correlation – there is no link between the independent and dependent variable. In this instance there will be no line.

Positive correlation – increasing the independent variable creates an increase in the dependent variable.

Negative correlation – increasing the independent variable creates a decrease in the dependent variable.

Linear – increasing the independent variable by a value increases the dependent variable by a constant multiple of that value.

Directly proportional – a linear graph that goes through the origin. Increasing the independent variable by a factor will increase the dependent variable by the same factor. Doubling the independent variable will always double the dependent variable.

Inversely proportional – increasing the independent variable by a factor will *decrease* the dependent variable by the same factor. Doubling the independent variable will always halve the dependent variable.

Does the line fit?

"But the line doesn't fit!"

It can be difficult for pupils to understand how to draw a line of best fit, especially if the correlation is weak.

A line of best fit is a straight line (or curve) that best represents the data on a scatter plot. This line may pass through some of the points, none of the points or all of the points. A straight line must be drawn with a ruler and can only go through the origin if those values have been measured or are known to definitely exist.

Use the following tips to help pupils draw an appropriate line and interpret it correctly:

- An anomalous result is a point that does not follow the pattern of the others points around it. Pupils should circle this and ignore it when adding their line.
- Using a transparent ruler allows you to draw a line without obscuring any of the points.
- The line of best fit should go more-or-less through the middle of the points. There should be roughly the same number of points above and below the line.
- Joining the dots is allowed, but only when there is uncertainty about the values in between. So you may take a temperature reading at noon for a month and plot by joining the dots. However, you cannot use the graph to estimate the temperature at midnight.
- If all the points are close to the line then the correlation is strong. If all the points are a long way from the line then the correlation is weak.

> **Bonus idea** ★
>
> Use strands of spaghetti to play around with a line of best fit. Curves need to be drawn freehand in one stroke. Make sure pupils rotate the graph paper to fit their hand's natural movement.

Fruit and sweets

"Chemical calculations – love them or hate them, they're here to stay."

Here are some very simple ways you can make this topic much more fun and stimulating. The crux is getting pupils to recognise that they already have the mathematical skills needed to succeed.

Use this fruit analogy for teaching GCSE chemistry calculation and link it to the basic maths skills. First make an image of a fruit bowl with a simple ratio of fruit, such as five apples, two oranges and three bananas. Ask what portion of the bowl is apples, and then what percentage. Then have a more complex ratio and do the same. The next step is to extend this to asking what mass of the fruit bowl is apples, with the cognitive leap being that you now need to know the average mass of an apple. The pupils can now work out the percentage composition of elements in compounds.

You can use sweets for balancing equations and also for calculating reacting quantities from equations. Start off with balancing some equations and move on to the reacting quantities later. Begin by talking about the ingredients required for baking a cake and ask questions such as 'If you need three eggs to bake a cake, how many can you bake with 30 eggs?' Then you can introduce some simple equations and begin to work out reacting quantities with the sweets before you move on to do it with masses of reactants and products.

It doesn't really matter which type of sweets you use, but wrapped sweets are always best. For simple equations using only two reactants and products, Maoam Minis are perfect!

Growth and decay

"Measuring what happens when something is out of our control – radioactive decay and reproduction of microorganisms."

You have probably spent time throwing dice and counting the sixes to model radioactive decay; how realistic is this model?

There are many different ways to model growth and decay. You can use wooden cubes with one side painted red, or just toss coins. Can pupils evaluate the authenticity of these methods and link the difference to half-lives? Try it with two different types of coloured balls or sweets. Let's say we have an equal number of red and green. Pupils take it in turns to remove a sweet from a black bag. After every ten goes you record how many reds are left in the bag, and produce a graph of this. Ask pupils to predict what will happen to the rate of removal of reds with time, and why this happens. For a higher-level activity you can plot the number remaining to investigate whether the model produces an exponential decay.

1, 2, 4, 8, 16, 32 . . . Yes, you can easily get your pupils to understand the increase in the numbers involved in bacterial growth, but do they understand how this changes over time? It is easy to graph this if pupils are given the time it takes for the number to double each time. It is possible to investigate this by counting colonies of microorganisms using this specimen ISA (Investigative Skills Assignment) from AQA: bit.ly/140Rzui

Chemists can get pupils to think about both growth and decay in terms of the consumption of reactants and the formation of products. Taking rates of reaction back to a mathematical concept is a good way to develop pupils' understanding of how concentration changes over time.

Taking it further

Try producing purely theoretical models as a spreadsheet with your pupils. You can successfully produce pH curves for a strong acid-strong base titration this way.

71

Modelling

Part 7

Modelling in science

"Getting pupils to visualise the invisible – enabling them to describe or explain phenomena that cannot be experienced directly."

Crates of Mallus is credited with producing the first globe in the second century BC, and the oldest surviving example of a globe is the 'Erdapfel' by Martin Behaim from around 1491. This is the perfect example of something we couldn't experience until the famous Blue Marble photograph of Earth was taken by Apollo 17.

There are two types of model: those that are a physical representation of something we cannot see with the naked eye, and those that test a hypothesis and make a prediction. Advances in technology have rapidly changed scientific modelling.

You will no doubt have physical models of some of the following in your school: DNA, molecular lattices, a human torso, the solar system, a central heating system, wave machines, slinkies etc. Make sure that your pupils have an understanding of the size and scale of your model, as mentioned in Idea 49.

Then you have fictional representations to address the more abstract concepts mentioned in your teaching, such as the different models of the atom and Galen's description of blood flowing as tides. There are also analogies to help visualise the abstract, such as the eye as a camera, enzymes as scissors, layered cake as sediments, the sun and planets as a nucleus and electrons, etc. In fact, chemical equations are themselves models that represent molecules we are unable to see.

The development of technology has enabled us to introduce much clearer models into our teaching. The PhET animations mentioned in Idea 8 are essential for all science teachers. One of the best examples of computer modelling, and a must for any climate change lesson, is the sea level simulator from flood.firetree.net/.

The choc cycle

"All kids love chocolate, and this is great, fun way of turning what can be a dreary lesson in to something all pupils will enjoy."

A fun practical activity that uses cheap resources to full effect. Even if you are struggling to engage a class during a rocks topic, you'll find that pupils will take over this lesson and you'll be able to wander round and support individuals.

Equipment – budget white and dark chocolate, cheese graters, washing-up bowls, glass bowls, plastic cups, rolling pins and foil.

Stage 1 – Start by getting pupils to grate the dark and white chocolate. Then sprinkle alternate layers of dark and white into a plastic cup, and use the end of the rolling pin to compress the layers. Pupils should be able to remove the 'sediment' from the cup in a single block. They may need to cut the sides of the cup with scissors.

Stage 2 – Put a few cm of hot water from the tap in the washing-up bowl and stand the glass bowl in it. It is crucial that the water is not so hot that it will melt the chocolate instantly. Place the layered chocolate in the glass bowl and allow it to soften. Press it gently with your fingers. Then allow it to cool and snap in it half.

Stage 3 – Replace the water in the washing-up bowl with hot kettle water, and stand the glass bowl in it. Put the chocolate in the glass bowl and let it melt. Pour it onto tin foil to cool.

Key questions:

What does the grated chocolate represent?

What is the rolling pin action representing?

Why are the conditions important for Stage 2?

How can you link the three stages to rock types and their formation?

What types of rock would a Lion Bar and Crunchie represent?

Teaching tip

Take the class to a food technology room for this lesson. They get to eat the final product at the end of the lesson!

Taking it further

Extension work – ask pupils to work out how to model intrusive and extrusive igneous rocks.

Lego

"Use this as a fun way to get pupils to show off and develop their kinaesthetic skills in science."

There are a multitude of different ways you can use bricks at any key stage and any topic. Here are some suggestions to get you started using Lego bricks in the classroom.

Teaching tip

If you don't want to buy potentially expensive bricks you can try all of the above with modelling clay. Both ways have their pros and cons, as do non-branded alternatives.

Lego bricks never fail to motivate pupils. Yes they may appear to cost a lot, but they will last indefinitely if you remember to check them back in vigilantly.

As a starter activity, give out some Lego bricks and ask the pupils to build something that represents something they learnt last lesson. Take a photograph of something you have built and ask pupils what they think it represents.

Use Lego to represent atoms, elements, compounds, molecules and mixtures. Get pupils to talk about how they develop the models and their similarities and differences.

Build Sankey diagrams using Lego! It's a great way of showing the principle of conservation of energy. Balancing equations also lends itself very well to using bricks. Just make sure you've printed out some crosses and arrows to go with the activity.

Older pupils could use bricks to represent the equations for photosynthesis and respiration. Pyramids of biomass and numbers can easily be built with bricks, too.

The more adventurous could use stop motion technology to make movies using the bricks. Use this in conjunction with the filmstrips from Idea 47.

The Edgerton Centre at MIT has a great page of resources using Lego to teach chemical reactions, photosynthesis and understanding air at bit.ly/100ideaslego.

Particle people

"A great, simple outdoor activity to get kids active and learning about the states of matter at the same time"

Pupils role play the motion and position of particles outside the classroom. You will need some space for this and some fat chalk to mark out shapes.

First, draw three concentric shapes on the ground outside using your fat chalk. You will need to gauge the sizes of these depending on the numbers in your groups. The inner shape is a cube. Around this draw a slightly larger droplet shape. The outer shape is a cloud; this should be much larger than the other shapes to represent the larger increase in volume of a gas.

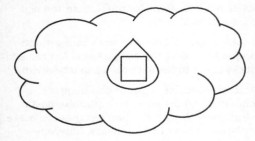

Start the pupils off in neat rows and columns inside the square. Direct the activity using command words such as solid, liquid, gas, ice, water, steam, faster, slower, compressible, boil, condense, freeze, melt . . .

Pupils should respond to your commands by moving into positions that represent the word. To ensure that pupils remain in contact while representing a liquid, instruct them to either hold hands or link arms with at least one other person at all times.

Follow this up with a literacy activity, with a focus on the command words used during the session.

Taking it further

Use a video camera so you can review the activity in the classroom later. This works even better if you can film from a high vantage point. Get the pupils to edit and annotate the video footage back in the classroom.

Pasta structures

"Sick of building bridges with craft straws?"

Here are a few different ways you can use spaghetti in the classroom. It's cheap, easy to snap and very strong. Have a look at idea 75 for something else you can do with cooked spaghetti.

Teaching tip

When making buckyballs, get pupils to make batches of hexagons in teams first. Help them out with this step by giving them a hexagon template to help control the angles and dimensions.

Many of you will have encountered the old team-building activities where you aim to build the tallest tower or the strongest bridge out of art straws. Here are some ideas for using spaghetti and sweets in a similar way. You can use marshmallows (or similar soft sweets) or polystyrene balls to connect your spaghetti.

Ionic lattices – make sodium chloride by using white marshmallows for the sodium and pink for the chloride ions.

DNA – pupils will need to work hard with the angles to achieve the double helix. You can add sticky labels to the base pairs and label them.

Macromolecules – pupils can begin by constructing diamond and graphite pasta structures. You could then get them to make different types of fullerenes. A fullerene is any molecule composed entirely of carbon, in the form of a hollow sphere, ellipsoid, tube or other shape. Spherical fullerenes are called buckyballs and resemble a football.

Here are some C-C bond angles to help:

- Diamond – 109.5°
- Graphite – 120°
- Pentagon – 108°
- Octagon – 135°

Those of you feeling more adventurous can introduce the formula:

Interior angle = $\frac{180(n-2)}{n}$, where n is the number of sides.

Lab organisation

Part 8

Lab organisation – top 10 tips

"A well-organised lab environment will make your life easier as well as the lives of the pupils."

Ten very basic tips to organise the running of your lab.

The smooth running of any science lesson always depends on you being organised and setting out very clear expectations of pupils. Pupils expect excitement, but you also need to exercise control.

1 Designated places for bags and coats.
2 Pictures of equipment on the cupboard doors.
3 If possible have the equipment spread around the room to avoid congestion.
4 Clear and positive lab rules on display. Make sure your lab rules are big enough to read from any seat – this should also apply to anything else you display.
5 Regularly check any health and safety equipment in the lab.
6 Consider using a one-way system during practical work.
7 To avoid distractions, display only purposeful materials on the walls.
8 Have seating plans you can display on your IWB.
9 Never underestimate the importance of your technicians and cleaners.
10 Have interesting items on shelves – make it look like a lab.

Remember, the lab is yours, for your pupils to use. It's a cliché, but a fact of life, that losing a class early on makes it harder to rein them in. Reinforcements, clarity and consistency are a must.

Don't forget, safety BEFORE learning every time.

Lab rules

"Always remember that health and safety comes before learning!!"

Here are some recommended lab rules. Create your own set within your department, basing them on positive messages.

The wording of any set of lab rules makes a big difference. Think about the difference between the following: 'You must never run in the lab' and 'Please walk at all times in the lab'. A positive message is much easier to reinforce. So here follows a list of top ten rules. Some schools may find it useful to have multilingual versions available.

1 All coats and bags in the places provided.
2 Walk around the lab at all times.
3 Listen when others are speaking.
4 If you aren't sure what to do next then STOP, READ and ASK.
5 Accidents do happen – make sure you tell your teacher straight away.
6 Drinking is not allowed during practical work.
7 Goggles must be worn when required.
8 Tie back long hair.
9 Clean spillages up as soon as they happen.
10 Safety FIRST, learning follows.

You set next week's expectations this week, and tomorrow's expectations today. It will be your patience, resilience and consistency that make your pupils safe learners. Have your rules displayed big enough for all to read and make sure you refer back to them periodically. Reinforce from the first day of year 7 that this is not a classroom.

Planning practical work

"Before you even plan a practical lesson you have to plan a practical that is purposeful!"

Practical work is the bread and butter of any science curriculum, and it is what defines its place in the curriculum. It is an advantage to have this sort of stimulus to help engage pupils of all ages and abilities.

You should always begin with the question 'Why are the pupils carrying out this practical?' It could be for the acquisition of either new skills or new knowledge. You can identify skills gaps quite easily by carrying out the practical audit in Idea 68.

You will get the most out of the practical part of the lesson if you:

- have ordered all the required equipment from your technicians and spoken to them about specific requests
- have tested any practical you are doing for the first time and spoken to experienced colleagues, who will usually have advice and be able to point out potential pitfalls
- introduce a clear and relevant context for the lesson
- make the lesson investigative and promote pupil ownership of the work
- avoid repetitive collection of data by promoting collaboration between groups – don't have pupils measuring rate at five different concentrations and ask them to collect repeat results
- are not afraid to demonstrate new skills and leave complicated equipment set out as WAGOLL; ask pupils to show you their equipment before they are allowed to begin
- avoid pupil-generated results tables unless this is a new skill

- invest a few minutes in taking equipment out of cupboards before the pupils arrive in the room
- consider introducing a one-way system around the room if there is a need for pupils to move back and forth many times during the lesson
- make sure pupils know exactly what to do with equipment and any waste at the end of the practical
- make a big point of counting out, or even handing out, specific pieces of equipment – there must be a crocodile clip graveyard out there somewhere
- use your whiteboard as a way of displaying diagrams of equipment and simple instructions, or, even better, for the recording of group results
- have designated wet and dry areas, particularly if using electronic devices during the lesson
- assign roles to pupils when they are working in groups of three or more – this will discourage disengaged spectators
- are aware of pupils with health or motor issues
- know how to stop a practical safely, including the use of your emergency shut-offs
- plan the role of other adults in the room and consider implications for their safety.

Taking it further

Don't be afraid to try something new. If you do, then invite other members of the department to join you after school when you try it out and make sure you understand any health and safety implications.

Bunsen burner licence

"All my Y7s have to earn their Bunsen burner licence during the first week of school to prove to me they can use it unsupervised."

This can be adapted for other science skills such as a microscope licence. I've also used a chemical handling licence effectively in the past.

It's the one question every science teacher hears from any new year group entering school – 'when do we get to use Bunsen burners?' Probably rightly identified as the most commonly used transferable practical handling skill, and one that also needs to be treated sensitively if you have any pupils with special needs related to motor skills. Get nice certificates made and make a big deal of pupils being awarded a certificate.

Your pupils can be assessed on the following:

- Name each part of a Bunsen and state what it does.
- Set up a Bunsen burner correctly – connected to the gas tap sufficiently, safe surroundings, and never under any equipment to be heated later.
- Light a Bunsen burner safely – with air holes closed and with a wooden spill that is extinguished after use.
- Use a Bunsen burner safely and be able to adjust the flame – be able to heat a solid object safely and to keep a beaker of water simmering.
- Safely put your Bunsen burner away – extinguish the flame correctly, allow to cool and put away in the correct place.

Don't be afraid to revoke the licence! You can cancel a licence at any time as a sanction for inappropriate or unsafe use. The pupil has to earn their licence back, either in class or in their own time.

Displaying pupil work

"With the advancement in emerging technologies there are many more ways to display pupil work than a traditional notice board or corridor display."

Get it out there as it happens! Some great ways to celebrate success instantly, to motivate and to share.

Visualisers – not very new technology, but getting better and better. Many have the ability to not only display work on your whiteboard but to save, annotate and share with other devices.

Twitter/Facebook – a great way to get examples out there, not only of great work but also of activities and experiences as they happen. Your school may have its own social media accounts, but why not set up your own science department Twitter account, or get school to add a Facebook page for your department?

Evernote – you can use a handheld device to grab a photograph of a piece of work and upload it to Evernote. If you have the same Evernote account visible on your whiteboard then as soon as you refresh the page the work will be visible to the whole class. You could take a photograph of a set of results and annotate with feedback. Similarly, you could put up a piece of written work and then collect post-it notes with suggestions for improvement.

School TVs – many of you will have these around school in key locations. Use them to showcase the best of your department.

All of the above are great ways of performing collective peer-assessment very quickly. They are also a strategy you could use for creating a portfolio of pupil work. Finally they are all an effective way of showing WAGOLL.

> **Bonus idea** ★
>
> Take your social media to a higher level by collaborating with other schools. Use Twitter and Facebook as a way of sharing results, photographs and videos. If it is used responsibly then you have a fantastic way of getting feedback from other pupils.

Inspirational quotes

"Wouldn't it be great if pupils could quote some famous scientists!"

So here goes . . . top ten quotes from scientists to display around your lab. NOTE: There is some debate as to whether the Einstein and Sagan quotes can be attributed to them!

'Give me a place to stand on, and I will move the Earth.' *Archimedes*

'If we did all the things we are capable of doing, we would literally astound ourselves.' *Thomas Edison*

'Everybody is a genius. But if you judge a fish by its ability to climb a tree, it will live its whole life believing that it is stupid.' *Albert Einstein*

'If I have seen further than others, it is by standing upon the shoulders of giants.' *Sir Isaac Newton*

'I would rather discover one scientific fact than become King of Persia.' *Democritus*

'Research is what I'm doing when I don't know what I'm doing.' *Wernher von Braun*

'Genius is 1% inspiration and 99% perspiration.' *Thomas Edison*

'Science progresses best when observations force us to alter our preconceptions.' *Vera Rubin*

'Somewhere, something incredible is waiting to be known.' *Carl Sagan*

Taking it further

Print a different quote each week/month as a banner and put it above your whiteboard. Use technology to display the quotes around school, or even as a desktop background on laptops.

'When one door closes, another opens; but we often look so long and so regretfully upon the closed door that we do not see the one that has opened for us.' *Alexander Graham Bell*

Why these particular quotes? They stimulate thought and discussion. Get pupils to work out exactly what they think each quote really means and then discuss it with their peers.

Essential visuals

"Labels, posters and signage will be abundant in a science lab – make them obvious and clear, and think about why they are there."

Think about what the essential visuals are in your lab, and how to make the most of limited space.

Let's begin with the obvious – hazard symbols, lab rules, school expectations, etc. All very familiar sights around any science laboratory, but what else do your pupils really need to know and how does their understanding of English hinder this understanding. Consider having the following in your lab:

Basics – pictures of bags, coats and books in relevant places around the room.

Equipment – pictures on cupboard doors and trays.

Taps – something obvious indicating where your hot water is.

Eye wash station – most are supplied with signage.

Hygiene – signs showing where hands are to be washed.

Goggles – signs reminding pupils they are to be worn.

Bags – if you have limited storage mark out a safe area of flooring with black and yellow striped tape.

Shelving – use labels to indicate where sets of books are stored. If they are textbooks, use a picture of the cover.

All of the above may seem like common sense, but they are all part of your default setting introduced in Idea 9.

Teaching tip

It may be useful to have the whole department decide on what is required and to have your technicians prepare, install and maintain these resources.

Great practical lessons

Part 9

Practical audit

"Why are you doing this practical work today?"

It's all about the skills pupils acquire, and identifying the gaps.

The 'Getting Practical' initiative was a professional development programme for science teachers, which has since evolved to become Practical Biology, Practical Chemistry and Practical Physics – www. nuffieldfoundation.org/teachers. One of the best parts of the initiative was the practical audit teachers carried out. Simply use the audit tool in the links below to identify the skills gaps.

- Develop knowledge and understanding of science.
- Learn how to use apparatus or carry out standard procedures.
- Develop understanding of scientific enquiry.

Primary audit tool: bit.ly/1m2yTNk

Secondary audit tool: bit.ly/1s7LPpU

To investigate the rate of reaction between sodium thiosulphate and hydrochloric acid at different temperatures, pupils use the knowledge that during the reaction the mixture goes cloudy as tiny particles of sulphur are formed. One way to conduct a practical investigation would be to ask pupils to collect results for five different temperatures, and also to repeat each temperature. An untrained observer walking past the lab would see a group of very busy pupils. But what are they actually learning? Doing the first measurement, they learn how to time the reaction until the mixture obscures a cross underneath it. The nine further measurements demonstrate no new acquisition of practical skills! How would you improve this practical?

Alginate worms

"A biological polymer looked at in a chemical context. This very simple experiment will captivate any class that sees it for the first time."

The cell walls of plants contain structural polymers. One of these is sodium alginate, which can be extracted from kelp and seaweed. The addition of food colourings makes this a very visual way of teaching cross-linked polymers.

Most people will probably be aware of the classic 'slime' experiment using borax and PVA glue to illustrate the change in properties when cross-links form. This version works much better and has much more visual impact.

You will need 5% $CaCl_2$ solution, Gaviscon or sodium alginate suspension, food colouring, two beakers and a pipette.

The beauty of this practical is its simplicity. All you have to do is add the sodium alginate to a beaker of calcium chloride solution. You can begin by letting it drop into the solution to form beads. Then you can put the tip of the pipette under water and squeeze the pipette as you move the tip through the solution.

So what's the science behind this? In the suspension, the singly charged sodium ions are bonded to the alginate chains. The calcium ions you add have a 2+ charge, so they can form bonds with two alginate chains, hence forming a cross-link between them.

Taking it further

You can make this more visual by adding different food colourings to your alginate suspension. See rsc.org/ Education/Teachers/ Resources/Inspirational/ resources/3.1.9.pdf and youtube.com/ watch?v=DeW3KYqX-tl.

The B of the bang

"A great fun lesson that leads pupils to evaluate three different methods for measuring reaction times."

This lesson is a great way of getting kids up and busy very quickly.

The lesson has three different methods of measuring reaction times, with a focus on the difference in the accuracy of each method. Begin with a video clip of a 100-m race and get the pupils to identify the key elements of the perfect race. Then discuss the concept of a false start and the tolerances allowed. It was Linford Christie who said he set off on 'the B of the Bang'.

Method 1 – Pupils join hands in a line. The pupil at one end starts a stopwatch and squeezes the hand of the next pupil. This continues along the line and back to the first pupil, who stops the watch. Calculate mean reaction time.

Method 2 – Pupils work in pairs. One pupil holds a ruler vertically in the air. The other stands ready to catch the ruler between their thumb and index finger. The catcher should line their thumb up with the 0 mark on the ruler, and use the width of the ruler to set the gap between their thumb and finger as a control variable. The holder should drop the ruler without warning, and record the distance it fell by reading off the point where it was caught. There are plenty of resources available online to find the reaction time.

Method 3 – Use the 'Sheep Dash' activity at bbc.in/MpKjPY, on laptops or the IWB.

With a larger class you could do the three methods on a carousel. Use the lesson to focus on evaluative skills, where pupils consider the merits of each method. Get your pupils to compare each model, and have a focus on key investigative skills such as their understanding of precision and accuracy.

Taking it further

You can repeat Method 1 with eyes closed, and even try it before and after drinking caffeinated drinks. The lesson context could be changed to investigate the placebo affect if you use decaffeinated drinks.

Beak adaptations

"... the singularly large number of the species of this sub-group in this one small archipelago (may help to explain) the perfectly graduated series in the size of their beaks." From the journal of Charles Darwin

Students love this very simple modelling activity designed to show how beak size and shape hels birds to adapt to the available food supply.

Use this idea when you are looking at variation within, and then between, species. Pupils attempt to pick the chocolate chips out of cookies using different types of tweezers.

You will need the following: disposable paper bowls, budget chocolate chip cookies, a variety of different tweezers, stopwatches.

Start by handing out the equipment; the students will quite happily evaluate the effectiveness of the different tweezers at removing the chocolate chips. You can then develop it into a competition where pupils are timed to see how quickly they can remove a certain number of chips from a cookie. You can also try a variation using dried peas mixed with rice. Even better, use a bag of mixed pulses and grains and investigate which type of tweezer is best suited to each type of pulse.

As a follow-up activity, ask pupils to research different types of beak shape and link them to the work they have been doing. Which beak shapes are analogous to the shapes of the different types of tweezer?

> **Teaching tip**
>
> As a simple starter activity get pupils to match different types of kitchen utensil to different situations, for example slotted spoons for peas and a ladle for soup.

Festive favourites

"Some great ideas here for making your own Christmas decorations and other festive science activities."

Hopefully these Christmas science ideas will make those last few days of that long first term relevant and interesting.

Teaching tip

Plan these activities so anything pupils make can actually be taken home at the end of the first term. So make sure they have plenty of time for their borax snowflakes to crystallise and dry. Similarly, chromatography will also require drying time before being taken home.

Displacement Christmas trees – make a tree outline with copper wire and hang it by some string in silver nitrate solution. The displaced silver makes a lovely coating on the copper wire. You could make a time-lapse video for this, and for some of the other ideas.

Poinsettia indicator – there are always plenty of poinsettia plants around at Christmas. Make an indicator from them just as you do with red cabbage. The colour of a poinsettia leaf comes from anthocyanins, which are usually orange/red at pH3 and below, and green/blue/purple at high pHs.

Christmas Day cabbage – red cabbage is a traditional dish served at this time of the year. It is usually cooked with the addition of apples to maintain the red colour at a low pH. Leaving out the acidic apples tends to result in a not-so-appealing dark purple colour. If you cook your cabbage with the addition of some baking soda you get a yellow/green colour.

Borax snowflakes – this is a very easy experiment, but it requires a few days to obtain a dry snowflake. Make some basic snowflake shapes from pieces of pipe cleaner. Then suspend the shapes in warm concentrated borax solution. As the solution cools the borax will crystallise on the pipe cleaners. You will need a day or two for the snowflakes to dry out.

Pine cone flame tests – a fun way of illustrating flame colours. You can sprinkle your usual flame colour chemicals straight on to your pine cone or use a solution in ethanol. Once lit they can burn quite well – don't forget your fume cupboard!

Silver mirror decorations – make your own silver decorations using old glassware. Just do your usual Tollen's reagent reaction, empty the glassware and seal with a foil-covered bung.

Chromatography Christmas lights – make some light bulb-shaped pieces of filter paper and carry out some chromatography. Once dried these can be stuck over LED lights to make some lovely covers for the bulbs.

Orange oil – many of you will buy oranges or clementines at this time of the year. You need a candle at the ready for this. Simply squeeze the peel and you will release the flammable orange oil 'limonene' into the candle.

Pine tree aroma – bornyl acetate (an ester) and the isomers alpha and beta pinene (turpenes) are three of the many substances that give your pine tree its distinctive smell. You can get pupils to investigate other aromatic substances associated with this time of the year, such as those in chocolate, chestnuts and nutmeg.

The dreaded Brussels sprout – the bitter taste associated with these seasonal vegetables is due to sulforaphane. Some people have a very low tolerance to its bitterness.

Taking it further

Don't forget every science teacher's Christmas essential – your clamp-and-stand Christmas tree with lots of glassware filled with coloured solutions. Push the boat out and add some traditional decorations and LED lights.

Rainbow fizz

"I can sing a rainbow . . . But can you make one?"

One of my favourite experiments for kids to do at open days: very visual and crammed full of science at many levels.

A great way of introducing any of the following into a lesson: pH scale, indicators, neutralisation, density and diffusion.

Equipment: test tube rack, boiling tube, universal indicator solution, 0.1 M hydrochloric acid, freshly made Na_2CO_3 solution (34 g in 100 cm^3 of distilled water), dropping pipettes.

Three-quarters fill the boiling tube with the hydrochloric acid. Add a few drops of universal indicator solution to the acid and gently swirl to give an even red colour. Now leave to settle for a little while. Hold the boiling tube at a 45° angle and very slowly let some of the sodium carbonate solution slide down the side of the boiling tube. The sodium carbonate is denser than the hydrochloric acid so it will sink to the bottom. Add enough to increase the height of the mixture by 1 cm. Now place the boiling tube upright and observe what happens.

You should see the whole range of colours for universal indicator solution develop, from blue at the bottom to red at the top, as the sodium carbonate solution diffuses, slowly neutralising the acid. The reaction also fizzes slightly due to the CO_2 produced.

Taking it further

Try the reaction with colourless pickling vinegar and antacid tablets, or even see what happens to the rate of diffusion if you change the temperature of one of the solutions.

A variation on this experiment is to begin with agar gel containing universal indicator solution, and then to pour either acid or alkali on top of the set gel. This is a great one for carrying out some time lapse. You can take this further by investigating the rate of diffusion of different concentrations of acid or alkali.

A safer thermite reaction

"Letting pupils loose to produce an exciting visual reaction of their own is always a winner."

This practical allows pupils to experience a great displacement reaction without the dangers of the thermite reaction.

Nothing beats a good thermite reaction done by an experienced teacher to full effect. There are many exciting videos available showing large-scale thermite reactions; however, this activity enables pupils to see a similar reaction that produces plenty of light and smoke. The reaction is carried out on a heatproof mat and pupils light it with a hot Bunsen flame. The quantities don't need to be exact. Each pupil needs to mix together a couple of spatulas of zinc powder and copper oxide powder. They are best mixed by passing them back and forth between two pieces of paper. The pupils then make a line of the mixture on their heatproof mat and heat one end with a blue Bunsen flame. Once lit the reaction can be seen moving along the line of the mixture.

The copper can be isolated by reacting any unreacted oxides and zinc with 2 M hydrochloric acid.

Follow-up work for this reaction can include displacement reactions, word equations, symbol equations and redox. More challenging activities could include working out percentage yield from the amount of copper produced. There is also scope to discuss why this reaction is so exothermic and why it needs heat to start the reaction. Watch a video of the practical carried out by students at bit.ly/1k2dQ2h.

Taking it further

The more experienced could carry out the silver nitrate–magnesium powder demonstration for a spectacular ending – see Idea 87.

Spaghetti worms

"Sometimes pupils need to understand that science experiments might be carried out over long periods of time rather than in the space of a single lesson."

Pupils need to understand the basics of natural selection and the work of Darwin before carrying out this practical activity. You will also need to carefully plan the time needed to collect the results, maybe over a period of weeks.

Teaching tip

There is an excellent resource published by the Wellcome Trust called 'I'm a worm, get me out of here', with lots more detail about how to carry out this experiment, at bit. ly/1zNXXxD.

This activity is best carried out during the winter months, when birds are more likely to feed from the food you provide for them. The basic principle behind the experiment is to investigate whether garden birds prefer to eat a particular colour of 'worm'. These worms are simply short strands of spaghetti cooked in different food colourings. You can leave the pupils to decide on all the other variables involved such as length of spaghetti, intensity of colour, scattering density and location. You will need a location within the school grounds that is unlikely to be disturbed. If possible, set a webcam up to view the birds.

As a numeracy activity get the students to identify all the numbers and variables involved, and then get them to work out how to process and present the results. They will need to think about how many to test over the time allowed, and how many to test at once. They will also need to decide how they will put out the worms and count them later. What will they do with partially eaten worms?

You may also find that a period of training is needed for the birds, as they will need time to familiarise themselves with the set-up and this type of food. The investigation becomes more complex if you introduce the concept of breeding and how this affects the population of your worms.

Practicals to do at home

"Science is all around us, and you can easily motivate younger pupils by getting them to try some science at home."

Here are some great activities that pupils can do at home. Most importantly, they are all very safe to carry out.

Density of fruit and vegetables – get your pupils to investigate if different fruit and veg float or sink. As an extension activity you can ask them to see what happens to the results if they use frozen or cooked vegetables instead. You could also ask them to see if they can get a paperclip to float.

Dancing raisins – simply drop a raisin or peanut into a glass of fizzy drink. Ask your pupils to focus on describing, then explaining, what is happening.

Testing pH – send your pupils home with some universal indicator and a list of household items to test before an acids and alkalis topic.

Cartesian divers – really simple if you provide the pupils with a list of the simple equipment they will need. Try using this as a way of illustrating the compressibility of gases.

Musical instruments – asking pupils to invent a musical instrument is a great introduction to a sound topic. Get them to explain to others how the sound is produced by their invention.

Hovercrafts – four pieces of simple equipment needed: an old CD, the lid from a bottle of sports drink, blue tack and a balloon. This a great introduction to forces and friction.

Static electricity – a very simple experiment in which pupils bend water from the tap with a charged plastic ruler. Combine this with a challenge where pupils are asked to take a photograph of a charged balloon they have stuck to a wall or the effect it has on somebody's hair.

Teaching tip

Don't forget to have written instructions for your pupils to take home, as some parents will want to get involved in helping their children.

Investigative
science

Part 10

Working scientifically

"Define working scientifically. As a department, what do you come up with?"

The rebranding of scientific enquiry resulted in us suddenly requiring pupils to be working scientifically. Did anything change?

The 2003 QCA requirements for new GCSEs stated that candidates must be able to:

- devise and plan investigations, drawing on scientific knowledge and understanding in selecting appropriate strategies;
- demonstrate appropriate investigative methods, including safe and skilful practical techniques, obtaining data which are sufficient and of appropriate precision, recording these methodically;
- interpret data to draw conclusions which are consistent with the evidence, using scientific knowledge and understanding, whenever possible, in explaining their findings;
- evaluate data and methods.

The draft KS4 national curriculum for teaching from 2016 states that working scientifically is broken down into the following four areas:

- the development of scientific thinking
- experimental skills and strategies
- analysis and evaluation
- vocabulary, units, symbols and nomenclature.

But has anything really changed? Can you make the pupils feel like they are scientists? Lab books may seem old fashioned, but focussing on the scientific method and the processes involved will make pupils feel like scientists. Some schools can afford lab coats for pupils to wear during practicals; you could have class experts who wear a lab coat as a reward.

Differentiation through science investigations

"Investigative science should be the bread and butter of any teacher's series of lessons for almost any topic."

Pupils should ask their own questions about what they observe and decide which types of scientific enquiry to use to answer them. They should draw conclusions and use some scientific language to talk and write about what they find.

One of the simplest investigations involves a ramp and a toy car. Introducing different levels of thinking skills turns this into an investigation that can be taken all the way up to calculating efficiency – measuring the potential energy of the car at the start and its kinetic energy later. Here are a few questions you could begin with:

- Describe what happened . . .
- What could have happened if . . . ?
- Can you apply the method used to an experience of your own?
- Can you explain what must have happened when . . . ?
- How many ways can you . . . ?
- What changes to . . . would you suggest?

Now think of the outcomes a pupil could produce:

- List all the possible variables.
- Produce your own table for recording results.
- Describe what your results tell you.
- Turn your results into a chart or graph.
- Describe the link between the independent and dependent variable.
- Suggest improvements to the plan.
- Describe a context in which the science is relevant in everyday life.

The different degrees of cognition required for the questioning and outcomes mean this technique works with even the simplest investigations and can be used at any key stage.

Teaching tip

Some teachers may have the confidence to allow pupils to write their own questions and devise a hypothesis. Others could prepare a set of differentiated question starters that can be used for successive investigations.

Scientific method

"Are your pupils able to answer scientific questions without being led through the process by you?"

Let's imagine you pose the question 'Does salty water make pasta cook quicker?' and then you just sit back and watch your pupils arrive at an answer. What journey would they take?

The Arab scientist Ibn al-Haytham (695–1040) is credited with the origin of scientific method because of his focus on experimental data and reproducibility of results. The process in its simplest form can be broken down into question, hypothesis, prediction, testing and analysis. This can be expanded with these important modern-day additions: replication, external review and sharing of data.

Now back to the penny investigation. Look at the process as following these steps:

1 Question - 'How many drops of water can a penny hold?'
2 Do some research – pupils may find examples of results by others, suggested methods, etc.
3 Own hypothesis – they may arrive at an estimate, or could state that the quantity is affected by a particular variable they need to control.
4 Design and test an experiment (modify if required) – they may work out a particular way to drop the water on to the penny. At this point they should be thinking about repeatability.
5 Collect results and analyse. There should be a focus on the validity of their data and any patterns.
6 Do the results support the hypothesis?

Yes – communicate results.

No – revisit hypothesis.

#5minprac investigation plan

"A great starting point for pupils embarking on a practical investigation. Perfect for controlled assessment at GCSE."

An introduction to the #5minplan series to help students begin to formulate a plan for an investigation.

The #5minplan by Ross Morrison McGill, aka @TeacherToolKit, is featured in *100 Ideas for Outstanding Lessons*. The #5mineval compliments it, and here is the #5minprac plan for students.

Give this out to small groups and get them to work together to identify a way of testing a given hypothesis.

Hypothesis – decide on what you are investigating and how your independent variable will affect the dependent variable. Pupils can be given a hypothesis to investigate, or the more able may devise their own.

Variables – identify your independent, dependent and all the possible control variables.

Context – how is this science relevant in the real world? For example, a scenario where a football stadium is upgrading its floodlights to higher-voltage bulbs would give context to an investigation into how voltage affects resistance. The installers would need to know how the resistance of the wires would change and if this would cause the wires to overheat.

Sources – the details of the sources you have chosen to inform your plan. Pupils require the skill of comparing sources they are given.

Equipment – a list of what the students think they will need to carry out the investigation.

Planning – the steps involved in writing their actual plan, with guidance for the key points, including a risk assessment.

Teaching tip

You may have an identified focus for your lesson, for example variables. Using this resource means that pupils don't spend a big chunk of the lesson writing, and they can focus on the skills. It is designed so they can plan an approach as a group from the outset.

Taking it further

Have these produced as laminated A3 resources if you plan to use them often. The advantage of the laminated resource is that it allows the pupils to make amendments to their work. There is more guidance about how this can be used at bitly/1nipZLa.

Penny investigation

"The simplest ideas can often generate the best lessons."

This is an open ended investigation in which pupils are asked the following question: how many drops of liquid can you get on a penny?

Equipment: selection of coins from 1p up to 10p, small beakers, washing-up liquid, ethanol, orange juice, apple juice, vegetable oil, plastic pipettes, salt, sugar, balance (optional).

The investigation is beautiful in its simplicity. Pupils count the number of drops of liquid you can place on the surface of a penny before it overflows. Here is a list of suggestions for the independent variable you could investigate:

• coin diameter
• type of liquid
• water:ethanol ratio
• concentration of solute
• number of drops of washing-up liquid in a volume of water.

Pupils may question the validity of drop size as a measure for the dependent variable. You could measure mass of liquid instead by carrying out the investigation on a balance.

This is an example of a pupil-led investigation. You can allow the pupils to decide on the variable they would like to investigate and just let them run with it. The focus needs to be on the process rather than the scientific concept. Only the more able or older pupils will be interested in surface tension. There is also a good combination of continuous and discrete variables possible in this investigation, allowing you to focus on line graphs and bar charts.

Making tea on Everest

"A great demonstration that shows how the pressure above a liquid can affect its boiling point."

More of an exercise in observation than a demo, but it's fascinating and rare that any pupil can explain what is actually happening before their eyes.

Take a tall jar with a metal lid (e.g. a passata jar) into which you can fit a whole thermometer. Fill it absolutely to the top with freshly boiled water and seal firmly with the lid. Get a student to monitor the temperature. Place ice cubes on the lid. After a few moments the water will start to boil again, usually well below 100°C. Keep adding ice cubes and the water will continue to boil, even though the temperature will drop. What is the lowest temperature at which you can keep the water boiling?

The explanation is that cooling the lid creates a partial vacuum underneath it. With the lower pressure the water will boil at lower and lower temperatures. At the 8848 m summit of Everest, water would boil at 71°C due to the reduced atmospheric pressure of around 34kPa.

You can use this very simple demonstration in many situations. It's a great extension activity to generate some creative thinking at KS3 as well as a good discussion starter for older pupils. Encourage pupils to research how the boiling point of water changes with atmospheric pressure.

Teaching tip

Set this as a problem-solving activity, as it will undoubtedly create some cognitive conflict.

Hydrogels

"A fun way of investigating hydrogen bonding and cross-linking of polymers."

Hydrogels are found in disposable nappies and hair gels. This lesson also links with Idea 69.

The absorbent substance in disposable nappies is the polymer sodium polyacrylate. It has the ability to absorb up to approximately 300 times its own mass in water. In its raw form the polymer chain hydrogen bonds to itself, causing the chain to curl up. When water is added, the water molecules replace the internal hydrogen bonding and the chain uncurls. This causes a huge increase in overall volume. The product looks like artificial snow.

You can buy sodium polyacrylate easily, as it is often marketed as 'magic snow', or you can just purchase cheap own-brand disposable nappies and remove the powder inside. A good demonstration is to add about a teaspoon of the powder to 50 cm^3 of water in a small beaker. If you experiment with the volumes you can get the beaker to overflow with the resulting huge increase in volume. Pupils can investigate how much water a fixed mass of polymer can absorb, or even which brand of nappy is the most absorbent. You can then get your pupils to carry out further research on the potential uses of hydrogels. There have been suggestions that they could be added to the soil in hot countries to slow down the evaporation of water. You could even attempt to grow plants in hydrogels.

Taking it further

To investigate further you can take some hair gel and add some salt solution to it. Get pupils to research the effect of adding the salt in terms of bonding.

Marshmallow catapults

"Loads of physics and a sporting link to shooting in this great problem-solving activity."

Another team-building and/or problem-solving activity that is good for teaching forces and energy transfers at any key stage.

This activity has been around for quite a while and there are some high-quality resources to accompany it available from the National STEM Centre eLibrary at stem.org.uk/rxb4n.

Equipment: 7 large lollypop sticks, elastic bands, plastic spoon, marshmallows, a measuring tape.

The activity involves building a catapult that will launch the marshmallow as far as possible. Stress that the final product needs to be free-standing and operated with one finger only. There is plenty of opportunity to discuss energy transfers. Younger pupils could look at the conversions into the kinetic energy of the marshmallow. Older students could discuss the kinetic and potential energy and even take it as far as efficiencies. A more advanced activity could use light gates to measure the speed of the marshmallow as it leaves the catapult!

As a starter activity you can use images or video clips of crossbows, trebuchets and catapults to stimulate ideas. You will also need a launching area with a measuring tape set up somewhere in your room.

> **Teaching tip**
>
> Buy large lolly sticks called craft sticks for bigger and better catapults.

Simple investigations

"We don't do much investigative science because we don't have the time or the equipment!"

Imagination is the only barrier to overcome! These are all tried and tested activities and they have been used during training sessions with up to 50 teachers as a carousel activity.

Here are some very simple, yet effective, starting points for investigations that can work from early years up to GCSE. You can use these stimuli to get teachers to design their own investigations with readily available materials. Think about the practical audit from Idea 68 and use this to help you to identify the skills addressed from each of the activities below. Remember to consider how pupils will record and present their results from these investigations.

- Rubber band, ruler, carrier bag, marbles or blocks, and a Newton meter if available.
- Cells, wires, bulbs, sticky tape and if possible a multimeter.
- Potato pieces, beaker, balance, stopwatch.
- Toy car, plank of wood, protractor, sticky tape, pile of pennies and a pile of textbooks.
- Bowl of water, regular fizzy drink, diet drink, orange, apple, lemon, boiled egg and raw egg.
- Kettle, beakers, salt, sugar, thermometer, stopwatch.
- A selection of balls, meter ruler, different materials as surfaces.

Work in groups to design your own investigations and then customise them. The planning posters at bit.ly/100ideasinvest are a very useful resource. Another strategy is to let the pupils play with the equipment and come up with questions themselves. For the toy car activity they will come up with ideas involving speed and hopefully realise that it is hard to measure.

Evaluating sources

"What makes a good source to help you plan an investigation?"

The major exam boards require pupils to carry out some research. These key questions will help your pupils evaluate the usefulness of each source.

- Does this source identify appropriate independent and dependent variables to test your hypothesis?

This will help pupils ensure that they are able to test their hypothesis.

- Does this source mention any control variables?

Pupils need to understand that if they are not aware of, or do not control, these variables then their results will not be valid.

- Does this source give a clear, step-by-step method?

This is a sure-fire way of helping to get high marks in the planning stage.

- Does this source mention any potential risks or safety measures?

Make sure that pupils have broken this down into three parts: the hazard, the risk it poses, and how to minimise the risk (control measures). For example: Risk – bus, Hazard – hit by moving bus, Control Measures – use a crossing, take headphones off, etc.

- Can the investigation suggested by this source be done with the resources available to you in a science lab?

This prevents pupils designing hypothetically excellent investigations that they are unable to carry out. It is always easier for them to evaluate their own methods rather than those given to them.

Teaching tip
Give the list of questions to pupils as credit card-sized checklists so they can attach them to copies of the sources they have used during their research.

Amazing displacement

"You can't beat either a good flash or a bang to grab the attention of your audience."

Venturing to further extremes of the reactivity series in this dramatic demonstration shows the full effect of differences in reactivity. This demonstration came from a Royal Society of Chemistry publication and it's a must for KS3 reactivity or KS4 metal extraction lessons.

Typical displacement or reactivity lessons often include very safe reactions carried out by pupils. The reduction of copper oxide with carbon or, for the more adventurous, reduction of lead oxide using blowpipes seem to be the usual class practicals. My 'Christmas tree displacement' in Idea 72 is a much better class practical. The thermite reaction tends to be the staple demonstration, but this takes it to another level.

All you need for this experiment are silver nitrate powder and powdered magnesium. You very carefully grind up the silver nitrate powder with a mortar and pestle. You then mix the two powders by passing them back and forth between two weighing boats or similar. *Under no circumstances* are the two powders to be ground together, as any friction will cause the mixture to ignite. You then place the mixture on a white tile or heatproof mat. Set up a burette of water so that it drips at intervals of ten seconds. Then move the burette into position over the mixture, and step back!

Another suggested way to start the reaction is with a drop of water on a glass rod attached to a metre rule.

The demonstration is also an excellent way of illustrating the effect of particle size on rates of reaction.

Boiling water in a paper bag!

"Rarely do I get a class that believes my claim that I can do this."

This is an original and intriguing way of demonstrating the thermal properties of water. Okay, it's not really a paper bag, but the concept is the same.

First you need to brush up your origami skills and learn how to make a paper cube. You can watch a video tutorial at bit.ly/1HihxrX. It is also possible to carry out this demonstration in a disposable paper cup.

Start by showing the pupils how easily paper ignites. Then set the demonstration up on a tripod and gauze. Try to use a simple, plain gauze for this. Make sure you test the demo in advance and work out the best flame setting. You don't want to ruin it by burning the paper, although paper doesn't burn until it reaches over 200°C. When it works well you get a plume of steam escaping from the vent at the top, and when it goes wrong the bag collapses, so make sure people are at a safe distance! You can hang a temperature sensor in the water to monitor the increase in temperature.

You can use this demonstration when teaching conduction to illustrate how well water conducts the heat and prevents the paper bag from burning. You can also discuss convection currents and why a kettle boils all the water, not just the water surrounding the element at the bottom. It's also a great introduction to specific heat capacity.

Taking it further

You can also hold a match under a water-filled balloon to illustrate the same principle.

Collapsing can

"A classic demonstration illustrating air pressure and the difference in volume between liquids and gases."

We don't even notice the pressure of the air around us. The reduction in pressure of the steam condensing within the can makes the air pressure collapse the can.

All you will need for this excellent demonstration is an empty aluminium drinks can. Prepare a large bowl of water first. Put 15 ml of water into the can, stand it on a tripod and gauze, and let it boil. Then pick up the can with some tongs, invert it, and then slowly lower it into the water and watch it collapse.

You can follow this up by discussing the particle model of liquids and gases, and it's a great way of illustrating the difference in the spaces between the particles. Another discussion can be around the difference in the pressure inside and outside the can. Often pupils will talk about astronauts exploding in space due to the difference in pressure, but is a scientific myth!

For a much more advanced lesson at A level, you could get pupils to work out the reduction in volume when 330 cm³ of steam condenses. They should easily be able to use the ideal gas equation to calculate the number of moles of steam and therefore how many moles of water this represents. Don't forget that the steam is at 373 K. You should get 0.0106 moles and 0.19 g or 0.19 cm³, so it easy to see the massive reduction in volume when the steam condenses.

Taking it further

You could try this with a larger can, or even a jerry can if you have a large bin available for the water.

Flaming rainbow

"Great for fireworks time of the year."

A simple demonstration of flame colours that can take you all the way to discussing excited electrons.

All you need for this are small evaporating basins containing metal salts dissolved in methanol. Make sure you are wearing gloves when you handle the methanol. A dark room will produce the best effect, and the liquids can easily be lit with a splint. The following metal salts will be needed to produce your rainbow of colours:

Teaching tip

A set of direct vision spectroscopes will make the flame testing much more interesting and help you introduce a higher-level understanding of light and colour.

- Red – Lithium
- Orange/red – Calcium
- Orange – Sodium
- Green – Barium
- Blue/green – Copper
- Blue/violet – Caesium

The key question is 'How does the heat energy produce the different colours?' The energy causes an electron to be promoted to a higher energy level called the excited state. The electron then falls back down to its ground state, resulting in energy being released as a photon of light. The frequency (v) of the light corresponds to the energy change (E) when we use $E=hv$, where h is Planck's constant.

As a follow-up you can get pupils to carry out flame tests using metal salts on clean nichrome wires. The wires can be cleaned by dipping them into concentrated hydrochloric acid and heating before use. You can also check out one of the festive favourites from Idea 72, where you can carry out flame tests on pine cones.

Licopodium powder

"A dramatic way to demonstrate the effect of surface area on rate of reaction."

A small pile of licopodium powder cannot be lit with a match; however mixing it with air provides a completely different outcome. Licopodium is the dry spores of clubmoss plants, with a size of around 33 micrometres (μm), and is traditionally used as a flash powder.

Teaching tip

Practice is the key to this demo, and it is great for open days. Make sure you have plenty of space and a high ceiling!

This is a very simple demonstration but you will need to make sure you have perfected your technique before the lesson. Begin by placing about half a teaspoon of the powder on a heatproof mat. Then try to light the powder with a match. The pile may darken slightly but will not burn.

Now for the fun part. Place a small pile of the powder, about 1 cm in diameter, on your hand just at the base of where your forefinger and second finger meet. You may need a helper for the next part. Hold your hand out in front of you and place a lit match upright in the middle of the pile. You should be able to grip it between your fingers. Slowly raise your hand so it is level with your shoulders, and then quickly drop your hand back down. As the powder falls out of your hand it mixes with the air and instantly ignites. You could use a simple explanation of combustion to explain the lack of visible products.

You need to make sure that your powder remains dry as any moisture will affect its flammability. An alternative method is to place a Bunsen burner on the floor and make a square around it with safety screens. Then drop the powder into the square from above. This method also works well for other materials such as custard powder.

Make your own comet

"Bring something from outer space into the classroom."

If you have access to dry ice then you can make your very own comet in front of your pupils.

Equipment: large mixing bowl, large bin liner, large plastic sheet, 5 kg dry ice, 1 litre of water, 2 cups of dirt/soil, 1 tbsp syrup, smelling salts, heavy-duty gardening gloves, large wooden spoon and a mallet or large hammer.

You must wear goggles and the gloves at all times. First begin by protecting the floor with the large plastic sheet, and then crush the dry ice into powder. Then follow these steps.

1 Place the bin liner into the mixing bowl.
2 Add half the water and the dirt.
3 Add the crushed dry ice and stir.
4 Add the syrup (organic material) and the smelling salts (amino acids).
5 Continue stirring and add more water slowly. You should get lots of 'smoke' given off at this point.
6 Finally, compress the mixture into the bottom of the bin liner, and then turn out on to the desk.
7 If you have time, leave the comet to set for about ten minutes.

You will probably need to try this a few times until you get the right consistency at the end. This much CO_2 will increase the levels in an average-size lab. It should be within a safe limit, but as a precaution make sure the room is adequately ventilated. As your comet melts you may see small jets of CO_2 escaping from holes that appear in the ice. This happens to real comets but on a much larger scale.

Teaching tip

This ties in nicely with the landing of the Rosetta mission and the landing of the Philae probe on Comet 67P/Churyumov–Gerasimenko in November 2014; see rosetta.esa.int/.

Methane explosion

"Exciting ways of burning methane; some bright, some loud."

Here we have two different ways of demonstrating the combustion of methane safely in the lab.

Method 1 – Methane bubbles

Add some washing-up liquid to a bowl of water. Get yourself a nice long piece of rubber tubing to connect to your gas tap and use it to create a layer of bubbles on the surface of the water. You can quite safely ignite the bubbles you have made with a splint on the surface of the water. The braver of you may wish to scoop some bubbles into your hand for lighting. Another way is to throw your handful of bubbles up into the air and light them with a splint on the end of a metre rule.

Method 2 – Exploding can

This is commonly done with an empty custard tin, but you can do it in an empty round sweet tin, like the ones you share with your class. First put a hole about 5 mm in diameter in the centre of the lid. Then make a hole in the centre of the base large enough to fit your tubing. Place the tin on a stand and fill the tin with gas. You can usually smell the gas coming out of the lid of the tin once you have flushed the air out. Now light the gas at the hole in the lid and stand back. As the methane burns at the hole in the lid the volume of methane inside the tin reduces, sucking air in through the hole in the base. The methane:air ratio will slowly decrease until it reaches the optimum level. At this point the mixture will explode and the lid will fly up. During the demonstration the flame may be very difficult to see and as it gets closer to exploding it may appear to have gone out. Do not approach it to check

Taking it further

A nice variation of Method 2 is available from the Nuffield Foundation's Practical Chemistry website at bit.ly/WLZY1m.

Monkey and the hunter

"A classic open-evening demonstration that isn't used enough in the classroom."

This is a fascinating open-day demonstration. The parents will be just as fascinated as the pupils!

This is a very effective way of showing how an object thrown horizontally falls at the same rate as an object that is simply dropped vertically. Introduce the demonstration with this question: What hits the ground first, a cannon ball you drop or one that you fire horizontally? You could try different variants of the same question such as throwing or dropping balls off a tall building.

You can find full details and a video of how to set up the demonstration at bit.ly/WQeAx4. The 'monkey' is held up in the tree by an electromagnet. When you fire the 'bullet' at the monkey it breaks the circuit and the monkey falls at the same time you fire the bullet.

Questions to ask during the lesson:

- What happens if we change the speed of the bullet?
- What happens if we change the mass of the bullet or the can?
- What other factors may affect the motion of the objects?
- What would happen on the moon?
- How could the monkey escape the bullet?

Don't forget that this will also make an excellent maths lesson. The supporting material from the National STEM Centre resources includes a link to the mathematical concepts and equations of motion that explain this demonstration.

Teaching tip

This also works really well in the dark if you can attach some LEDs to the can and the bullet. It makes videoing the demonstration much more interesting!

Screaming Jelly Baby

"From 'unclaimed babies' in 1864, to 'Peace Babies' in 1918, to 'Jelly Babies' in 1953 and now 'screaming Jelly Babies' in the classroom."

Possibly one of the most popular secondary school demonstrations. Designed to let students see and hear how much energy there is stored within a Jelly Baby, and give them a better understanding of energy released during respiration.

Teaching tip

Enthalpy of combustion of glucose is -2805 kJmol^{-1}, so 100 g of Jelly Babies should release approximately 1558 kJmol^{-1}. Get students to discuss the difference between the two values and have the nutritional information from the pack at hand.

This is such a simple but effective demonstration. It is loud, visual and exciting! All you need is the following: boiling tube, boss, clamp, stand, 15 g potassium chlorate (V) and a Jelly Baby. Jelly Babies can be used because they have a small enough surface area for the reaction to take place at an appreciable rate, without being explosive. Make sure you adhere to safety precautions. The demonstration must be carried out in a very well-ventilated room; preferably point it towards an open window, and *never* do it in a fume cupboard. There is excellent guidance about how to carry out the demonstration available from the RSC here: rsc.li/1FMfOLj

Ask students to estimate how much chemical energy is stored in one Jelly Baby, and then try to contextualise this. For how long would a 100 W light bulb work with this amount of energy? How much energy does a person need every day?

Some facts about Jelly Babies: 100 g contains 73.8 g of sugars, predominantly from the sugar and glucose syrup. This translates into 1421 kJ of energy according to the nutritional information on the packaging. You could get pupils to research how far you could walk from the energy released from one Jelly Baby.

This is CLEAPSS Hazcard 77; there is further guidance available from rsc.li/WR3Tub.

Exam preparation

Part 11

Effective revision strategies

"Seems like common sense to say that the best starting point for revision is knowing what to revise. It's what comes next that is the key to effective revision."

Pupils find it easier to recall work that has been consolidated during day-to-day teaching, but curriculum time often prevents this from happening as often as needed. Identification of the gaps is key at this point.

If your exam board provided an enhanced results analysis, this should be your starting point. It can help you to identify not only the content areas but also any confusion arising from misinterpreting command words, the most common being describing rather than explaining and vice versa. Once you have your evidence, the next step is to develop ways of addressing the issues.

Start with question walk-throughs. Without addressing the actual question, get the pupils to tell you what they can interpret from the information provided in the question. Quite often they will now have the answer. You could follow this with Idea 100.

Try using pupil experts. This will involve setting homework where students work on different parts of a topic, thus becoming an expert in that area. As part of their homework get them to write questions about their specialist area. Once back in the classroom the experts take turns to present to and then question their group.

Deconstruct past papers so they address skills as well as content. All exam boards address Assessment Objectives (AO), but do your pupils know the difference between them? Plan an exercise where they label the questions to indicate which AO is being tested.

6-mark questions

"In this question you will be assessed on using good English, organising information clearly and using specialist terms where appropriate."

Put lots of practice in to this type of question. Make sure you have them embedded into your normal day-to-day teaching material.

Not only is science knowledge and understanding assessed in a 6-mark question, pupils are also assessed on their quality of written communication (QWC). Below are the criteria the three major exam boards publish.

AQA

- Ensure that text is legible and that spelling, punctuation and grammar are accurate so that the meaning is clear.
- Select and use a form and style of writing appropriate to the purpose and to complex subject matter.
- Organise information clearly and coherently, using specialist vocabulary when appropriate.

PEARSON (EDEXCEL)

- Present relevant information in a form that suits its purpose.
- Ensure that text is legible and that spelling, punctuation and grammar are accurate, so that meaning is clear.
- Use a suitable structure and style of writing.
- Use specialist vocabulary when appropriate.

OCR

- Ensure that text is legible and that spelling, punctuation and grammar are accurate so that meaning is clear.
- Present information in a form that suits its purpose.
- Use an appropriate style of writing and, where applicable, specialist terminology.

> **Teaching tip**
>
> Each exam board publishes their generic marking requirements for a 6-mark question. You may like to consider having one in every exercise book, or a laminated class set to give out.

Command words

"How do you expect to be able to answer the question if you don't know what the question is asking you to do?"

There has been a much higher profile for command words in recent years, and many teachers are very familiar with them. Here are some common strategies and pitfalls.

Every exam board publishes its own list of command words with their meanings for GCSE sciences. The focus here is on those common to all major exam boards.

Calculate – work out a numerical answer. This will usually include having to show your working out and the units. Remember marks can be awarded for both of these.

Compare – describe or identify the differences and similarities between things. You would expect to see connectives in answers such as 'bigger', 'heavier', 'more than', 'quicker', 'less expensive' and 'however'.

Complete – this will require pupils to add words, labels, points on a graph, a mean in a table or perhaps electrons on a diagram.

Describe – facts about what happens, perhaps in the correct order. (Not to be confused with 'explain', which is why or how!) This type of question is usually about an experiment or a 'sequence of events' in a logical order. A good gauge to the amount of detail required will be the number of marks awarded.

Evaluate – take the information provided and your own knowledge to discuss and come to a judgement. This type of question goes beyond 'compare'. Expect to see pupils using similar connectives and then weighing up the facts at the end.

Explain – writing about how or why something happens. This needs to be more than just a list of reasons. There will also be a logical order to the explanation. You would expect to see 'because' in the answer.

State/Write down/Give – very simple answers that are often one word or perhaps an equation. This could also be a question where pupils are expected to label a diagram.

Suggest – application of knowledge to a potentially new situation. You'd expect to see words like 'could', 'I think' and 'might' in answers.

If you look in more detail at the common command words there is a hierarchy of thinking skills required.

• Knowledge – state
• Comprehension – describe, explain
• Application – suggest, calculate
• Analysis – compare
• Synthesis
• Evaluation

Interestingly, synthesis seems to be missing from the words the boards have in common. However, it is easy to argue that pupils are often required to write a plan for a procedure.

Taking it further

Have posters around the room with command words clearly displayed for pupils to see. For GCSE you should be able to identify the command words you will find in higher papers and not in the foundation papers.

C.U.S.T.A.R.D.

"A great acronym that can be used to help your students nail that 6-mark question!!"

A couple of years ago I came across a great acronym to for students to use as a checklist for their 6-mark questions. It's easy to remember and can make a great visual for your classroom wall.

Training your pupils to jump through exam board hoops is inevitable, and the importance of getting these 6 marks cannot be stressed enough. It could make the difference of almost a whole grade.

You can start off with some copies of old exam questions that you have laminated. Get the pupils to use dry-wipe markers for letters C to S. Then use whiteboards for T to D.

- **C**ircle the command word (see Idea 98).
- **U**nderline the key words.
- **S**cribble down extra words that may be useful.
- **T**hink it through and try to make sense of the key words.
- **A**ccount for every part of the question.
- **R**ead your answer back to yourself.
- **D**o not rush.

You should get photographs or copies of pupils' work and make a set of exemplars to use in class.

Annotated questions

"Take the pupils beyond being just answerers of exam questions to being teachers of exam questions."

This strategy is a great way of enabling pupils to begin to think more like an examiner and to add much more detail to their answers. When finished the work can be laminated and put up on a learning wall in your department.

Start by copying exam questions on single-sided A4 paper. These copies will be cut up to be used for the next step. Now provide the pupils with A3 paper to produce their work on. They should answer the exam questions, cut them out, and plan how to set the pieces out on the A3 paper. Now hand out some speech bubbles and ask the pupils to use these to justify their answers to the questions. Alternatively, you could just get pupils to draw bubbles on the A3 paper, but this limits the opportunity to correct mistakes.

A simple example would be a very low-demand question where pupils are matching pictures of specialist cells with the names of specialist cells. Once a root hair call has been correctly matched the annotation may say 'fine hairs provide a large surface area for the absorption of water and dissolved nutrients'. A red blood cell may be annotated with 'concave shape increases surface area for absorption of oxygen and has no nucleus'.

You can also use the speech bubbles to stretch pupils further. Have a selection of pre-prepared bubbles and then get pupils to write a matching question and answer.

Use this with pupils who lack confidence when writing answers. You will find that once pupils have done this with lower-demand questions they will try more challenging questions.

References

Idea 1: Collins English Dictionary

Idea 12: *Horrible Science: Shocking Electricity* by Nick Arnold and Tony De Saulles

Idea 12: *Braniac Science Abuse* (TV show)

Idea 14: https://royalsociety.org/~/media/education/policy/vision/reports/vision-summary.pdf

Idea 30: *Back to the Future* (Robert Zemeckis, 1985)

Idea 31: *Science and The Simpsons* by Simon Singh

Ideas 34, 80: *100 Ideas for Secondary Teachers: Outstanding Lessons*

Idea 38: 1 A vision for Science and Society – Department of Innovation, Universities and Skills 2008 (bit.ly/100ideaslit)

Idea 38: 2 American Association for the Advancement of Science (AAAS) (1993) Benchmarks for Science Literacy. Project 2061. Oxford: Oxford University Press

Idea 78: www.gov.uk/government/publications/national-curriculum-in-england-science-programmes-of-study